Haunted Charlotte

Haunted Charlotte

Supernatural Stories from the Queen City

ROY HEIZER
Photography by Nancy Heizer

4880 Lower Valley Road • Atglen, PA 19310

Dead~ication

This book is Dead~icated to the spirit (and spirits)
of the people of Charlotte.

It is also Dead~icated to Jeff Metz,
for his time and effort on this collection of stories.

Copyright © 2014 by Roy Heizer & Nancy Heizer
Library of Congress Control Number: 2014950220

Black Steam Looking Like Smoke On White Background by Geo-grafika.
Vintage paper background by melis. Courtesy www.bigstockphoto.com.

All rights reserved. No part of this work may be reproduced or used in any form or by any means—graphic, electronic, or mechanical, including photocopying or information storage and retrieval systems—without written permission from the publisher.

The scanning, uploading and distribution of this book or any part thereof via the Internet or via any other means without the permission of the publisher is illegal and punishable by law. Please purchase only authorized editions and do not participate in or encourage the electronic piracy of copyrighted materials.

"Schiffer," "Schiffer Publishing, Ltd. & Design," and the
"Design of pen and inkwell" are registered trademarks of Schiffer Publishing, Ltd.

Cover design by Molly Shields
Type set in Porcelian & Adobe Caslon

ISBN: 978-0-7643-4703-0
Printed in The United States

Published by Schiffer Publishing, Ltd.
4880 Lower Valley Road
Atglen, PA 19310
Phone: (610) 593-1777; Fax: (610) 593-2002
E-mail: Info@schifferbooks.com

For the largest selection of fine reference books on this
and related subjects, please visit our website at www.schifferbooks.com.

You may also write for a free catalog.
This book may be purchased from the publisher.
Please try your bookstore first.

We are always looking for people to write books on new and related subjects.
If you have an idea for a book, please contact us at proposals@schifferbooks.com

Schiffer Books are available at special discounts for bulk purchases for sales promotions or premiums. Special editions, including personalized covers, corporate imprints, and excerpts can be created in large quantities for special needs. For more information contact the publisher.

Acknowledgments

The City of Charlotte
Mecklenburg County, NC
Historic Rosedale Plantation
www.historicrosedale.org
NODA Arts District
Charlotte Area Paranormal Society
www.charlotteareaparanormal.org
Mecklenburg Historical Association
www.meckdec.org

The author would like to tip his hat to
Anders Manga and Devallia Anders of the band
Bloody Hammers, as well as to Adam Neal for their
friendship, support, and inspiration.

Coffin of Contents

1. The Icy Intersection . . . 7
2. The Returning Ghost . . . 14
3. Michael . . . 19
4. The Charlotte Mansion . . . 24
5. The Gentleman Janitor . . . 33
6. Dr. Narishkeit . . . 38
7. An Amended Sense of Happiness . . . 44
8. Mr. & Mrs. Benson . . . 51
9. Like a Lunatic . . . 55
10. In The Forest . . . 58
11. A Stroll Around the Neighborhood . . . 64
12. Homeward Bound . . . 70
13. A Relentless Spinning . . . 77
14. Clock & Watch . . . 81
15. Ginger's Bridge . . . 93
16. Winter . . . 99
17. The Factory . . . 102
18. Fred Mirkoff . . . 108
19. The Lincolnshire Hotel . . . 113
20. Mrs. Aberley . . . 119
21. A Resentment . . . 124
22. The Corpses . . . 125
23. Elderberry . . . 129
24. Aunt Sally . . . 131
25. The Old Elmwood Cemetery . . . 137
26. The Playmate . . . 140
27. Rosedale Plantation . . . 145
28. The Shotgun Houses . . . 154

Conclusion . . . 157
Spooky Gallery . . . 158

1
The Icy Intersection

In the early 1930s, 4th Ward was a sleepy little bedroom community on the northwestern side of the Queen City. With rolling hills, a thriving downtown, and four distinct seasons, 4th Ward was a nearly perfect place to raise a family. It seemed like everyone knew everyone and the 4th Ward neighborhood was a tight-knit community. The area had less than 1,400 people in those years, and while it was a tranquil bucolic town, the city leaders were quick to see new opportunities for growth and expansion. 4th Ward's history was a success story from the start, and the area quickly boasted a bustling downtown district, thriving businesses, and growing neighborhoods. It was an ideal Mid-South American community, but, despite being exemplary, it was no less subject to the tragedies more often associated with larger cities.

In 1933, America was steadily recovering from the Great Depression, and the 4th Ward neighborhood was leading the charge. Shopping centers, warehouses and churches were being built, the business area was thriving, and jobs were available. Several busses were purchased by a newly formed bus company to transport the growing population to the suburbs. Out-of-work men from all over North Carolina and Virginia came to 4th Ward looking for good jobs along the foothills.

One of those men was Thomas Miller, who brought his family down from Danville, Virginia, to the Charlotte area. Thomas took a job at the

Haunted Charlotte

The Icy intersection as it appears today.

1: The Icy Intersection

large general store on Fairview Road. Due to his honest, hardworking nature, he was quickly promoted to manager. His wife, Katherine, a stay-at-home mom, took in work making, repairing, and altering clothes for the neighbors. She was both liked and trusted by the other women in the neighborhood. They often brought their own children over to play with the Miller kids while having their clothes repaired.

The Millers and their three children, Tommy, Delbert, and Allison, joined the local Presbyterian Church and they all began to make friends and settle into their new lives in the neighborhood. Tommy and Delbert were as close as two brothers could be, both in age and friendship. The two boys were only a year apart and so the two of them felt more kinship than rivalry. They had their moments, but by all accounts, Tommy and Delbert were friends for life. Allison Miller was three years younger than Delbert, and while she mostly made her own friends at church and school, she did occasionally come along with her brothers on their outings.

On Tuesday, January 14, 1936, Delbert celebrated his tenth birthday. Two days later, Tommy celebrated his eleventh birthday. While Thomas and Katherine gave each boy a small present on his respective birthday, they were, in fact, planning a surprise birthday party for the following Saturday, January 18. The Millers had spent the week asking other neighborhood parents if their children could come over and join the celebration.

Saturday arrived in 4th Ward, along with a heavy blanket of snow and sharply colder temperatures than the previous week. When the two boys awoke to the snow-covered hills, they could hardly contain their excitement, but their mother beckoned them to stay inside for just a little while longer. She finally convinced them to eat a late breakfast in the kitchen, and throughout the mid-morning meal Mrs. Miller was busy delaying the boys' escape from the house for as long as she could. In the meantime, Mr. Miller was busy in the living room preparing for a birthday party. He set out a table, blew up a few balloons, and hung some streamers. He set out the cake that Mrs. Miller had baked in the middle of the night. When all was ready, he motioned at the front door to the neighboring house, where several friends of the boys were waiting to come to the birthday party.

Unable to keep the boys in the kitchen any longer, all convened in the living room to the joyous singing of "Happy Birthday to You." The boys, along with Allison and the invited friends, jumped and danced around the room. With songs sung and cake eaten, it was time for one mutual present to be given to the boys. A mutual present had become a Miller family tradition, and that year it was a large handmade wooden sled. Tommy looked at the sled in wonder, while Delbert jumped up and down shouting, "Thank you, thank you, thank you" as loud as he could. Several of the boys' friends said, almost in unison, "Let's take it out for a ride right now!" and the birthday party quickly spilled out into the cold, snowy day.

The children took turns running and jumping onto the sled and sliding down the street. For more than an hour the children played with the sled, throwing snowballs at each other in between turns on the new toboggan. It was the best present two young boys could get.

Soon though, the sledding adventure made its way to the hill near the corner of West 6th and North Church Streets. The hill along North Church Street, in those days, was steep and the newly fallen snow had made the hill irresistible to the group of children out sledding.

Bristling with excitement, Mr. Miller and the children gathered at the top of the hill. Tommy and Delbert climbed onto the two-man sled, crouched down, and prepared to be pushed off by one of the other kids. Soon, they were speeding down the street as fast as they could. With snow rushing past his squinted eyes, Tommy looked over the front of the sled, only to see the ice-covered street fly past him. Holding fast to Tommy, Delbert had his head buried in Tommy's back, while the frigid winter air flashed down around his collar. The children at the top of the hill chanted "GO, GO, GO" while waving their arms in the air. Mr. Miller watched with happiness and thought to himself what a great gift it had been—perfect for a chilly January day.

At that moment, though, the sled came quickly into view of West 6th Street. Even on that snowy, icy day, West 6th Street was filled with busses and cars and, at that exact moment, one of the newly purchased busses, driven by Clarence Dunmercer, was headed west down the road. Mr. Dunmercer, who had a spotless driving record, saw the sled speeding toward him. He made all the appropriate maneuvers, but fate had a more ominous plan. The bus and the sled crashed into each other a few minutes before noon, and when the bus came to a stop along the opposing curb, the mangled sled was under the front driver-side wheel.

Delbert had been thrown several yards by the force of the impact. He was badly bruised and shaken, but otherwise unhurt. Tommy, however, was not so lucky. He had been caught under the bumper and wheels of the bus, which had dragged him for more than forty-five feet. Nearly every bone in his body was broken, including his head and neck. In all likelihood, the coroner would later say, he never knew what hit him. Mr. Miller and the other children came screaming down the hill, some of them sliding down on their own. Mr. Miller screamed to the sky, while looking first at Tommy and then at Delbert. He reached Delbert first and bent to pick up his son, only to rise again and start calling for an ambulance. In an unimaginable state, Mr. Miller then went over to Tommy and, upon seeing his eldest son,

1: The Icy Intersection

The Icy Intersection is not far from the Presbyterian Church graveyard.

fainted with grief. Mr. Dunmercer was out of the passengerless bus, standing in the street wailing at the sight of the accident. Word of the calamity soon reached Mrs. Miller back at the house and she became inconsolable. The headline in the paper the next morning read: "Local boy killed in sledding accident."

A funeral was held for Tommy Miller and many people from around town came out to pay their last respects to the boy and his family. After the funeral, his body was taken back to Youngstown for burial. Delbert Miller eventually recuperated from his physical wounds, but the joyous boy was gone forever. Allison, a witness to the tragedy, seemed to be covered from that day on with a thin veil of happiness that hid her sorrow. The other children told varying accounts of the story, but all agreed it was the worst thing they had ever seen. Unable to cope with such a loss, Mrs. Miller asked her husband if they could move back to Youngstown. She just wanted to live someplace where she wouldn't have to be reminded of Tommy every time she left the house. They soon moved back to Youngstown and have since become lost to history.

The accident took only a few seconds, but a family and a town were changed forever. The bus company agreed to pay a settlement to the Millers and the bus involved in the accident was dismantled and sent to scrap. Mr. Dunmercer, overcome with remorse, apologized to the Miller family repeatedly. He quit driving and left 4th Ward. Slowly, the tragedy began to fade from the townsfolks' memories and things went on as normal in 4th Ward.

Ten years to the day later, on January 18, 1946, 4th Ward, North Carolina, was in the middle of a warm spell. Temperatures all over town were in the mid-fifties. The town of 4th Ward had only grown larger in the years since the tragedy and the street was filled with people that unusually warm day when a scream split the town's regular routine. A woman who was new to 4th Ward had passed out in the street and a large crowd gathered around her. When she awoke, she claimed that she had witnessed an accident. She claimed that she saw a bus hit a little boy. She was quickly assured that no accident had occurred that day, but she was told of the prior decade's tragedy. Several longtime locals remarked that she must have seen the ghost of the nearly forgotten Tommy Miller, but she quickly denied seeing a ghost, claiming a momentary lapse of perception. She had simply misperceived a common traffic situation. Her husband came to take her home and the commotion died down.

The next day, the woman who the day before had seen the vision, was again on West 6th Street when she saw something. This time, though, it was not an accident, but a somewhat translucent figure of a young boy

1: The Icy Intersection

dressed in play clothes and covered in blood and snow. She stood there at the intersection of West 6th and North Church Streets and watched as the ghastly looking boy circled the intersection. Soon, as she watched, a car drove through the intersection without stopping. She watched in amazement as the car simply drove right through the boy as he stood there staring off into space. Hadn't the driver seen him? Why had he kept going? Did the driver not feel the impact? In near hysterics the woman chased the car down the street, catching up to it at the next intersection. She pounded frantically on the car window until the driver rolled the window down. Upon screeching to the driver about the boy in the intersection, the driver got out and the two of them looked over the car and the street. Nothing unusual was there, although the driver did say to the woman that he had sensed a strange icy chill he could not explain while driving through the middle of the intersection.

The woman was checked into the local hospital for a rest, so hysterical that she could not even tell the doctors her name. Once she had an opportunity to calm down, the doctors asked her about the hallucinations she experienced in the street earlier that day. She had no explanation. At first, her experience was whispered about around town and most people wrote her off as crazy, until more and more people in the neighborhood began to see the ghostly figure of a bloody snow-covered boy in the intersection.

Many people, over the years, have claimed to have seen the ghost of Tommy Miller in that intersection. Not just in January, but year round. In August of 1962, an elderly couple claimed that, while driving through the intersection of North Church and West 6th Streets, their car briefly appeared to be covered with snow and blood. When they pulled over to inspect the car, it was clean.

While claims of ghostly sightings along that section of North Church Street have subsided in the years since 1946, even today, some still claim that they can see the ghostly presence of Tommy Miller as he searches for his lost toboggan.

2
The Returning Ghost

As Claude Dourdaine slept peacefully, his wife, Silene, stirred uneasily next to him in bed. The Grandfather clock in the parlor downstairs had just struck three o'clock in the morning when the hinges on the back door began to squeak. From all the way upstairs, Silene heard the door scrape the threshold as it was forced open. Fear nearly engulfed her as she realized someone was in the house. Heavy footsteps crept deliberately across the kitchen floor, down the hallway, and into the parlor. Silene frantically nudged her husband awake and he quickly sat upright in bed as he came to consciousness.

Silene whispered to Claude, "I hear someone near the front door." While trying not to upset his wife, Claude wondered to himself if it might not be their fifteen-year-old son getting something to eat, or perhaps slipping out to have some late night fun with his friends.

The front door creaked open and slammed shut. The sounds disappeared and the house fell silent.

Claude got up and quietly looked in on their son, who was fast asleep in his bed. Next, he went downstairs, only to find the front door still locked tightly from the inside. All the windows were closed and locked, with their panes intact. Claude went to the kitchen door and found that it, too, was securely locked. Yet, someone, or some*thing*, had walked through their house

2: The Returning Ghost

The house next door to the empty lot.

that night; both he and Silene had heard the footsteps as clearly as if they had been in the same room. It was no dream; they had both heard the intruder.

In the morning, Claude and Silene agreed that there must have been an intruder, even though the doors were locked. Ghosts, after all, can walk through doors, they surmised. A ghost would have no need to unlock a door. Ghosts, too, float, having no means of creating footsteps through a house. Yes, it must have been a human intruder…ghostly though he seemed.

The next night the incident reoccurred. The following night the ghost returned again, and the night after that, too. The intrusion was always at the same hour, right at three in the morning. Claude and Silene were both frightened; they had saved for a long time to buy the house in North Carolina, in the fall of 1913. Now it was late November, and in less than four months their dream home was quickly becoming a nightmare. The nightly intruder continued to appear through Christmas and into the spring of 1914.

On a number of occasions, Silene and Claude stayed up late into the night to try to see what, or who, was invading their home. Sometimes they could hear footsteps on the garden path near the kitchen door, but every time they looked out the window, all they saw was a peaceful garden in the moonlight. They never saw a trespassing intruder of any kind. Night after

Windows appear to glow in the twilight.

night, Claude would check the doors and windows after they heard the footsteps, but to no avail. The house was consistently secure. "Who is it?" they asked each other day after day. What apparition was walking through their home? As the nights went by, the Dourdaine's fear subsided little.

One day, in the summer of 1914, Claude went out of town on business. As he left, he promised Silene he would return in a few hours and that she would be all right. He tried to assure her that their son was a strong young man, and quite capable of helping his mother.

Silene sat restlessly in bed alone that night. She listened to the clock strike midnight, and then one in the morning, then two in the morning. The three o'clock hour was on its way and Silene was terrified to be in the house when the mysterious intruder came again. Nearly out of her mind with fear, Silene let out a scream to wake the dead when the three o'clock chime woke her from the lightest sleep. Right on time, she heard the kitchen door creak open. Silene knew she must confront it, to see it face-to-face. She pulled on her bathrobe and tepidly walked to the head of the stairs. In her fear, she forgot to look in on her son. She gazed down into the darkness of the stairwell as heavy footsteps moved across the floor downstairs.

Suddenly, out of the darkness, Silene saw a stout, wide man climbing the rough wooden staircase. He was coming right at her, but he seemed to

2: The Returning Ghost

Silene to be unaware that she was there. He wore rounded glasses that fit his rounded face. A large dark, untrimmed mustache framed his rounded mouth. A neatly tied green ascot slithered down from his face and quickly disappeared behind a silver silk vest. When the unwelcome gentleman came near to Silene, she fainted and fell to the floor.

Claude was at her side when she awoke, holding her tightly. As he listened to her story of the intruder, neither one of them could recall ever seeing such a man in or around their house. Claude checked the doors and the rest of the house. All was secure and they were alone. Not a lock or a petunia was out of place. Why their son had slept through the incident, Silene could not answer.

Claude knew only one way they were ever going to rid themselves of the unwelcome guest. The next night, he loaded his gun and sat at the kitchen table. Exhausted from a lack of sleep, he waited while his heart pounded blood through his veins. As the clock struck the three o'clock hour, Claude heard paces on the stoop just beyond the door; their ghost had returned! Though he could not see much in the dim light of the kitchen, he heard the lock unhook. As he heard the doorknob turn, he fired three shots through the door. He waited a long drawn-out minute for a reaction, but when none occurred, he opened the door. Moonlight and the smell of gunpowder was all that was there to greet him.

Claude, Silene, and their son moved out of the house the next morning. Over the next few months ghost hunters came to the house and held vigil, each hoping to get a glimpse of the returning apparition. Most people who came to the house could not stay awake until three in morning, and the neighbors soon began to complain about the strangers sleeping on the vacant lawn.

As the stale house drew no more sightings, eager spectators began to drift away to other, more interesting, sightings. The house sat empty for a time. It was eventually sold to a young couple from central Indiana, who told their agent that they were not scared of ghosts and that a "haunted house" might be somewhat amusing. It was not amusing for long. The couple lived in the house only a few weeks before departing for parts unknown.

The house sold several more times over the next few years, but none of the owners stayed long. All of them, it seemed, complained of the ghost that walked through the house at three in the morning. No violence or death was ever reported at the home, just a lot of sleepless nights.

Eventually, in 1923, the vacant house burned to the ground in a mysterious fire. As the fire chief and his deputy watered down the last of the smoldering frame, the fire chief leaned over to the deputy and asked "Do you know what time this fire was reported?"

"No," replied the deputy, "but if I had to guess, I'd say three in the morning."

The fire chief just nodded his head and went back to work.

Despite the fact that the house burned down and the lot remains empty to this day, some in the neighborhood still say they can hear footsteps at the sight every morning… just after three o'clock.

3

Michael

I grew up in the suburbs of Charlotte and spent my youth going to school and playing with friends. Charlotte, in the 1970s, was a great place to grow up. The city was thriving and yet the country was not very far away. It was a place of infinite possibilities and hard reality. My dad worked downtown among the office buildings with a view out over the rolling hills of Mecklenburg County. My mom retired from the Charlotte school system when she married and started to raise a family. My older brother had his friends, while I hung out with a group of four other boys and we were as tight as any circle of friends. We spent our free time playing basketball, riding our bikes, and walking in the woods. We slept over at each other's houses, traded baseball cards, stories, and dreams.

Albert Donald, Eric Korman, Eric Britain, Michael Stevens, and I were not only in the same grade in school, we were also in the same Boy Scout Troop and lived in the same neighborhood. Albert's dad was a police officer, while Eric Korman's dad was the head Rabbi at one of the area synagogues. I do not remember much about Eric Britain's parents, just that he was a precocious boy, full of energy and the one of us most likely to get into trouble. Michael's family was a little more complex than the other boys' relations were; his dad was quite a bit older than his mother was, didn't work, and was strangely vague. His mom said she was a student nurse at the local hospital. Something seemed odd about his sister, but she was rarely around. I remember the father telling me once that they had come to Charlotte from Los Angeles, California, so the mother could be in the nursing program. Michael, though, seemed to be the most normal one in his family; he loved to play and was as dedicated a friend as anyone could want. Michael Stevens just loved life and was willing to go along with just about anything we decided to do. He wanted more than almost anything to have a friend—and be a friend. Despite our being in this gang of five, Michael was my best friend.

Albert was the cautious one among us, reserved and orderly. He was the one who always wanted to play games that involved planning or math. Eric Korman was the curious one; he wanted to know everything about everything, and his favorite pastimes were reading and storytelling. On one occasion, the four of us who were not Jewish visited Eric Korman's synagogue and made fools of ourselves from our complete lack of knowledge about the Jewish tradition. Eric Britain was an athletic boy, wanting more to be on a basketball court than in a classroom. Eric Britain also had Tourette's Syndrome, which made for some interesting situations. One time we were all sitting around in a corner of the playground when a teacher came over to check on us. One by one, we said we were fine. When it came time for Eric to answer, he threw a Tourette's Syndrome fueled fit. The teacher, who knew about Eric's problem, just let it slide with grace and professionalism. Meanwhile, the four of us just giggled uncontrollably. While the five of us were different in some ways, we were also very congenial. We played and worked well together and the friendships lasted for years.

Then, in the late summer of 1980, my father was transferred. We were moving, and I was devastated. How far were we going to move? Would I ever see my friends again? Late into the evening that night my mother sat up with me, trying her best to assuage me. We were moving to Mooresville from our hometown of Monroe, a distance of only thirty-five miles, but it seemed like a million to me. Monroe is in Union County, while Mooresville is in Iredell County, which meant I would have to enroll in a new school and make new friends. While my older brother looked upon the move to Mooresville as an adventure, I was skeptical that things would work out for the best.

My mother assured me that I could continue to see Michael, Albert, and the two Erics if I wanted to, and the move was not as painful as it might have been. I started in a new school just over a week after we moved into the new house in Mooresville. As the school year went by, I saw less and less of Albert and the two Erics, but I made a real effort to keep up with Michael. The Saturdays I liked best were the ones when Albert or one of the Erics came over, too. On an almost weekly basis, I went over to Michael's house or he came to mine. My mother or father could always find some reason to go into the city on Saturday, and they would drop me off at Michael's to play for a few hours. Little by little Albert and the two Erics

3: Michael

The house believed to be the former Stevens's residents.

began to drift away; Michael and I saw them less as the months went by and, in the late fall of 1981, Michael told me he had not seen them in a while. He told me that Eric Korman was in Hebrew school full time and the other two were in different classes now.

The semi-weekly visits to Monroe continued, and although I was developing new friends in Mooresville, I still thought of Michael as my best friend. By the spring of 1982, Michael and I had developed a pattern to our visits. We would trade off months, and skip the third week each month. For the most part, this pattern worked well and our parents were glad to see us continue a friendship. For all of his family's oddities, they valued friendship and wanted to encourage us.

May was my month to go to his house, and so, on the first Saturday of May, I got up early to get ready for my visit with Michael. That week it rained all day and so we stayed inside and watched television, promising each other that the next Saturday we would play soccer.

The next Saturday came around and I got up early to pack my soccer gear. My father was waiting by the car when I was finally ready to go. We hopped in and set off on the thirty-five minute drive, leaving the house at around eight in the morning. My dad and I talked about the usual things that day and the trip went by quickly. Before I knew it, we were pulling into Michael's driveway. I ran up to the door and started pounding on it, but no one answered. My father was in the habit of waiting until I was inside to drive away and that time was no exception. I looked at my father and shrugged my shoulders. He told me to knock again, but still no reply.

He got out of the car, came to the door, and knocked for himself, and still there was no answer. My father was a curious man who could get tenacious about finding an answer. Had the Stevens family forgotten I was coming and gone off to do something else? Were they all still in bed? Had something else happened to them? Were they all right? My father and I both asked each other these questions while standing on Michael's front porch. While I waited on the front porch, my father began to look around the house. He peered into the first floor windows, and then went around the side of the house to look in the garage door windows. I waited nervously for him to return and tell me what was going on.

What he told me when he came back, I will never forget as long as I live. He told me that the house was empty, completely empty. There was not a stick of furniture, nor a person or a painting left behind. The house was clean, neat, and vacant. I ran around the house to have a look for myself and my father was right, the house was totally empty. Not only was the family gone, the dog had been taken away as well. Michael and his family were simply not there; they had vanished. Both my father and I were very confused; we had both been there one week earlier and everything was normal, as far as we could tell. My head flailed in confusion; my friend was gone. No letter, no phone call, simply gone.

My father went over to the neighbor's house and asked if they knew what had happened to the Stevens family. They did not know, although they did say that they were hardly ever home and a moving van might have come and gone without their noticing. They let us use their phone and my father called Michael's number. The phone company said that number had been disconnected and no forwarding number was available. My father tried several other neighborhood houses, but to no avail. No one knew what had happened to the Stevens family; they had disappeared like a sound in the night.

I was worried about my friend. What had happened to him and his family, why had they disappeared so quickly? My father was a bit of an amateur Sherlock Holmes and a mystery could entertain him for months, and while I worried, he investigated. He made several phone calls to people around town to inquire about the disappearance. He went to the school to try to talk to the principle; he thought that surely school records would reveal clues as to the family's evaporation. He got nowhere. My mother even asked around the PTA; no one knew anything. All the letters my mother wrote the post office returned with no forwarding address. The University

3: Michael

of Charlotte hospital said Mrs. Stevens simply did not show up one day when she was scheduled. The administrator that we talked to did say that Mrs. Stevens was only a couple of weeks from graduating. My father even went so far as to try to get Albert's father to start an investigation. Mr. Donald made some inquiries, but came up empty handed. The Charlotte police chief declined to open a full-scale investigation due to lack of evidence a crime had been committed. In fact, he could not find any evidence that the Stevens had ever existed. With a name as common as Stevens and a city as big as Los Angeles, further inquiries all led to dead ends. No phone records, no school records, and no employment records were ever disclosed. Neither Michael nor any member of his family was ever located.

How could an entire family completely disappear without leaving some clue?

4
The Charlotte Mansion

The exact location of the house escapes me now. It was, though, somewhere on the north side of uptown Charlotte. As I remember, it sat up on a hill overlooking some wandering old street, lined with aged trees and old hand-built rock walls. The house was Victorian in its architecture; it might even have been a painted lady—I really can't recall. Since that final frightful night, I've never returned.

It all started in mid-September; the air was slowly turning cooler and the skies were more cloudy than sunny. I was, in those days, a student at the University of North Carolina at Charlotte and I was living in student housing just a few blocks from the house. My roommate and I would go out and take walks around the neighborhood occasionally, and it was on one of these walks that we first came across the house. The first time I saw it, I thought it was fascinating and, even though I had no reason to suspect it then, a bit creepy. The gables seemed to float in a dreamlike manner, giving the house an aura all its own.

My roommate remarked that it looked empty and that it would make a great haunted house. If we had only known then what we know now, we would have left well enough alone and kept on walking, but, being young and curious, we decided to investigate it.

4: The Charlotte Mansion

The sun was beginning to set and light was quickly becoming scarce. We looked around to make sure no one was watching us as we crept up the driveway and peered into one of the side windows. The day's last sliver of light showed mostly empty rooms with just a few pieces of furniture. As we looked through the glass, we could tell that the house had not been lived in for a while and that it needed a good dusting. The furniture was not covered, however, and it did not look deliberately closed up. It looked more like it had been abandoned rather suddenly for some unknown reason. We slowly walked around to the back of the house and, as I made the corner, I was suddenly overtaken by a cold breeze across my shoulder. A piercing, yet indiscernible, sound drew my attention momentarily and I turned to look at my roommate, but he was nowhere to be seen. I quickly went back to the side of the house where we had first been, only to see my roommate running down the sidewalk in the direction of our apartment. I followed him, nearly tripping over a bucket as I went. While he ran, I walked at a fast pace that was somewhat slower than his.

On the way, I looked up from the sidewalk long enough to see another house along the route back to our place. It was dark by then and I couldn't see the house well, certainly not well enough to identify it now anyway. What I could see clearly of the house was a large bay window, well lit from the inside. Standing in the window watching me was a middle-aged woman with dark shoulder-length hair. I could clearly see her face in the light and I noticed she was pretty in an interesting sort of way. Maybe it was just my heightened state of excitement, but the woman seemed to stare at me intently for the length of time I was on her portion of the sidewalk. I got the distinct feeling she knew where I had been, and what I had been up to.

It was only after we were both safely back at our place and had recuperated from the running that my roommate explained to me what he had seen, or rather sensed, that had frightened him so. He told me that he had only been a couple of steps behind me and had stopped to peer into a cellar window, hoping to get a glimpse of anything that might have been under the house. Through the cobweb-covered window, he explained, there was a small vague light on in the basement. He said he tried to strain his eyes to get a better look, and that was the moment when, as best I can remember his description, it happened.

The faint light went out suddenly and, in that instant between the darkness of the room and his eyes adjusting to the outside light, he claimed that he saw or sensed a figure move ominously in the basement.

Had someone been there or was it just a young man's mind playing tricks on him? He could not say for sure. From what I remember of the incident, neither he nor I slept well that night. Being that I had a similarly weird experience, my roommate and I just decided to chalk it up to the exotic look of the house and the excitement of the investigation.

Over the next several days, my roommate and I did not speak of the house or the fright we'd each had in the course of looking the place over. Finally, I asked my roommate what he had thought of the house. He boldly answered that he had just pretended to be frightened to scare me and maybe have a laugh. So, I, being a somewhat obnoxious friend in those days, challenged him to go back to the house.

His stubborn macho attitude overcame his reason and he said, "Okay, I'll go back, but only if you go with me…we could even take a couple more guys just to keep a look out."

I remember feeling like I was becoming involved with some grade-school prank, but I said, "Let's go this Saturday." And our plan was set.

The next Saturday at last arrived, along with much cooler and cloudier weather. The strong scent of Halloween lurked in the air and the street was filled with the scraping sound of newly fallen leaves swirling about. While my roommate and I were willing to go in the middle of the day, the other two guys who had agreed to come along insisted that it be in the evening. Based on the description the two of us had given them, they wanted to see for themselves if the house was as creepy as we'd described it. At this point, they were brave, but I suspected, even then, that was going to quickly change.

Toting coats and flashlights, we set off to explore the old house around five in the afternoon. As the four of us made our way down the block, I noticed the mood in the small group had gone from grandiose excitement to something a bit more cautious. Along the way, I glanced over at the house with the big bay window just in time to see the curtain fall, as the shadow of the woman I had seen the other night disappeared behind it. Although I did not mention it to the other guys, I felt like she was watching us as we walked along the sidewalk. She had given me the shivers, but I quickly turned my thoughts back to the current expedition. As we arrived at the street where the house was, one of the guys— I can't remember which one of us—remarked that the sun was nearly gone and dark clouds were dominant over our heads. We made our way around the curve in the street and there it was before us: the house I have since come to call "The Charlotte Mansion."

Between the weather, our expectations, and the season, the house looked downright foreboding…and inviting. We knew we were trespassing, but the lure of the house was too much to resist and, so, we entered the yard. At first we stuck to creeping silently along the hedgerow, trying to hide our criminal activity as best we could. It was only after we had made our way to the top of the hill and mostly out of view from the street that we attempted to explore the house out in the open. Though I doubt any of us, at the time,

4: The Charlotte Mansion

would have admitted it, we were each scared—of the house, and, of being caught trespassing. I was nearly overcome with frights I'd never sensed before or since, but none of us wanted to be the one to wimp out, and so we pressed on with the investigation. I mean, a dare was a dare after all.

As we looked around the house, both together and separately, over several long minutes, the four of us each, as I recall, began to feel a strange mixture of wishful curiosity and amplified terror. Some time passed as I looked around the front porch on my own, careful to not be seen from the street. As my outstretched fingers pressed into the cracking shedding paint on the front porch floor, I pushed my nearly paralyzed body up to each window sill to get a look inside. As my eyes made it past the glazing of the first window pane and fully into the glass, I could, at first, see nothing. With nearly agonizing patience, I allowed my eyes to adjust to the darkness of what surely must have been the living room, but that night only eerie shadows cast life into the room before me. I collapsed into a sitting position on the porch, my back awkwardly pressing into what at last occurred to me must have been a nail sticking out of the clap boards. When I reached behind me to manipulate whatever it was I drew back only a few drops of my own blood. "Damn," I remember thinking: "I've torn a good shirt." "Oh well," I thought, "it'll be proof that we were here."

I must have passed out or drifted off into my mind's imagination in some way, because the next thing I can remember is one of the other guys screaming in a prolonged shrill manner that I immediately took as serious. It jarred me back to something like reality and I struggled to my feet as quickly as my aching bones would let me.

As I remember, I darted my eyes around in the half moonlight as my roommate came slowly into view. He was, I'm sure, covered in cobwebs, dirt, and sweat from his own investigations in another part of the house.

"Come quickly," he said, "Mike has been hurt."

The two of us made our way in the moonlight to the far side of the house where we found Mike laying in a pile of the autumn's first golden yellow-colored leaves. Upon seeing Mike splayed out prostrate on the ground, I cautiously looked up the old, crooked ladder he had obviously been climbing on, to try and catch a glimpse of where he might have come from. At the top of the ladder was a window, a nearly dark window. I quickly noticed a faint glow around its frame, a glow that could only have been made by some sort of lamp or candle—or so I thought.

Upon making sure that Mike was all right, I began to climb the rickety ladder against the advice of my roommate. I remember him asking me not to climb the ladder; I remember, in fact, he also asked if we could just call the whole thing off. The other guy with us—Doug, I think that was his

Haunted Charlotte

Now a restaurant, this Mansion has a secret past…

name—came up at that moment. He was just in time to smirk at my roommate, presumably for wanting to split. Looking back on it now, we should have listened to my roommate, but my curiosity had been re-peaked by the window at the top of the ladder.

    I climbed slowly up the ladder, making sure to adjust my balance as I went along. Doug, I think, held the ladder steady from the ground. After several minutes of cautious ascension, I had made my way far enough up the ladder to get my first look into the cracked and dirty window. There was a glowing light in the room all right, but that was the only clear thing I can remember seeing. The light, though only faintly glowing, made the rest of the room unviewable from the outside.

    At last, Mike, feeling better by that time, said, "Well?"

    I looked down the length of the ladder at him and said, "I can't really see much from here beyond the dim light coming from the room." I climbed back down the ladder with trepidation and relief. I gathered my nerves and said to the others, "Guys, we have a choice to make: we can either call it a night, or we can go inside and see what the reason for that light truly is."

    Each of us stared at the others for what seemed like an eternity. None of us wanted to be the one to say, "Let's go home." There was really no conversation, no choice…just four college kids and their egos and sense of

4: The Charlotte Mansion

immortality. We gathered our wits and made the decision that the back door would be the best way in, as it was most out of sight from the rest of the neighborhood. Like nervous sentries on watch, we made our way over to the back door. The night had fully come upon us now and the small back porch was completely dark, lit only by the occasional flash of a car or truck's headlights fracturing through the hedgerow and reaching us as we stood at the door.

Doug pulled out a flashlight, so we were able to see the door more clearly. Some dust had settled on the door's molding, but otherwise it looked normal.

Mike suddenly said, "I'll do it! I'll be the one to get it open."

I guess after his embarrassing fall from the ladder, he had something extra to prove to us. He tinkered with it, pulled and wiggled the handle, and banged his shoulder up against it once or twice. Soon, the door came open and Mike took his hand off the handle and let the door go. The door swung slowly open on its own, as if some invisible butler was opening it from the inside. It slid all the way back until it quietly came to rest on the empty coat hooks behind itself. I must say now, against our better judgment, we entered.

The house was almost completely dark, with only the stray outside light casting shadows across the walls. We had, of course, no plan of action. We did, however, agree to meet in the attic after each one of us had done some exploring on his own. We spread out to search the house. Doug and my roommate were the only ones with a flashlight, and that left me and Mike to investigate the rooms empty handed. Mike and I started our exploring together, but quickly split up, as I wanted to go one way and Mike another.

I can only say what I saw next, as the other guys were in other parts of the house. As I remember now, I did not see anything out of the ordinary. I did notice that while the basic furniture was there, what you might call "personal items" seemed to be missing. I did not see, for example, any toothbrushes in the bathrooms, no family pictures in the living room, no pets or houseplants. Only shadows in the darkness. As I made my way through the first floor and up to the second, I occasionally heard the footsteps of one of the other guys. Occasionally, too, I saw the beam of a flashlight. I worried about some outsider being able to see the flashlights from the street below—perhaps the woman in the big bay window had followed us and was watching us—but I figured we'd taken our chances by being here in the first place. Besides, the weather outside was chilly and cloudy; chances were slim that anyone would be outside anyway. Still, though, I worried. To my amazement, the other three guys were unusually quiet and discrete, making only the irregular gasp or awe.

Haunted Charlotte

At long last, I had made my way to the foot of the attic steps. The faint light peeking through the crack in the attic door let me know that I had arrived. The attic light was the only one in the house, and so slight was its illumination that it barely made its way down the attic steps. As I stopped to appreciate my surroundings, I was suddenly overcome with a feeling—a weird, unexplainable feeling. So powerful was the turning in my stomach that I had to reach out and grasp the door frame to keep from falling over. I cannot to this day say whether it was real or just a symptom of my fright or guilt at our trespassing. After several painful moments, I regained my composure, just in time to see Mike and my roommate come around the corner. That was three of us, but Doug was still missing. We had agreed to wait for all of us, and so we each exchanged our stories of exploration while we waited for Doug. After what was most likely only about ten minutes, but which seemed like years to us, we decided to go up into the attic space without Doug.

I led the way this time, with Mike and my roommate not far behind. Slowly and cautiously I made each step ascending up the flight of stairs. I recall expecting one of the others to say something like, "Hurry up, you slowpoke!" But they kept as quiet as a graveyard on a winter's day. By the time I made my way up the stairs enough to split the light, an oddly shaped shadow cast itself across the attic floor right in front of my eyes. The shadow appeared to be an elongated human figure. *Doug?* I thought. Had he made his way up to the attic before the rest of us?

As my eyes adjusted to the strange light and my sense of smell settled on the scent of cedar, the attic's full breadth unraveled before me…or had it?

When the final steps had been climbed and we were all in the attic, the three of us just stared around. Unlike throughout the rest of the house, in the attic, we all stayed together. We made our way across the shadows on the floor, ducking to miss the roof beams. Even though the calendar said the second of October, the heat of the summer still clung to the attic air and I began to feel stuffy and cramped. The atmosphere, both figuratively and literally, was getting to the other two as well. My roommate pulled off his coat and laid it over the back of an old chair. Mike wiped his brow and remarked that it was awful hot for that time of year, even though the rest of the house had been unusually cold. As we moved to what we thought was the front of the house, we came closer to the source of the light. I don't remember if we looked through the items in the attic or not; the next thing I remember was passing by the rather large brick chimney that came up through the floor and went up into the roof. As we passed the chimney…

4: The Charlotte Mansion

there it was. Lying in the faint light, I'll never forget it as long as I live... and maybe even after that.

The corpse, the dreadful prostrate corpse that lay before us sent us reeling. Whether our nerves will let any of us recall it or not, we all moved backwards, gasping in fright. Mike even hit his head on one of the roof beams, nearly knocking himself out in the process. And then...like a ghost in the darkness, Doug appeared out of nowhere, giving us a second fright that nearly put an end to the three of us.

Doug just laughed. He laughed the kind of laugh that only the dead can laugh. He reached out to me, but his arm just seemed bizarrely translucent in the half light of the attic. My mind reeled and raced with every thought I'd ever had. Was it a joke? Was it real? Was it my frightened mind playing games with me in the company of the dead? Where was I? What was happening? I screamed—I'm sure I screamed; what else could I have done? I tried to force my mind back to something like reality...only to see Doug's face. I didn't know Doug all that well; he was one of Mike's friends from campus. Why, in that briefest of moments, as I stood there with trembling knees did Doug look so familiar? I quickly looked away, only to look down again at the corpse on the floor. And there, to my horror, was Doug. I looked back up only to see Mike and my roommate standing there.

All memory of what happened next eludes me now; the next thing I remember, I was running down the sidewalk toward our apartment. Running down the sidewalk past the house with the bay window, a window I did not have the nerve to look up at. That is all I can recall from that night. My roommate and I, at my request, never spoke of the incident again.

Though that is all I can recall from that night, that is not the end of the story. It was about three years later and I had graduated, moved south to Rock Hill, South Carolina, and taken a job. In Rock Hill, I started to date a young lady named Janet. She quickly became the love of my life and, after only a few weeks of dating, I began to think about marriage. One night, she told me that her father had died some years prior, but invited me to meet her mother and some other family if she could convince them to join us. We made, as I recall, a reservation at a local restaurant and the date was set.

A week later, on the night of the reservation, I got dressed up in my Sunday best and headed out to meet Janet and her mother. I have to admit I was a bit nervous; I mean, this was going to be the girl I was going to marry and I certainly needed to have at least met her mother. As I walked into the restaurant, I saw Janet already seated. I saw another woman, whom I assumed at the time to be her mother, although her back was turned to me. The waiter nodded pleasantly to me as I approached the table, and he extended his arm out to show me the way to the two ladies. Although I did not appreciate it, or even think about it at the time, the waiter did look familiar to me. As I arrived at the table, Janet's mother looked up at me and my blood ran cold. Janet's mother was the woman in the big bay window. Although I had only briefly seen her back then, her face was as seared onto my memory as my own face. My mind was instantly awash with terrifying memories of "The Charlotte Mansion." The corpse, Mike, my roommate, Doug, the light, the nail, all came back in a flood of thoughts. As I turned to run from the restaurant, I saw the waiter, with his bizarrely translucent arm outstretched toward me, pointing the way to the door. I ran out through the door into a rainy night. I never saw Janet, or her mother, again.

5
The Gentleman Janitor

Somewhere along Graham Street, heading out of Charlotte, there stands a nondescript two-story brick and plate-glass office building. Rectangular, sturdy and insipid looking, the building blends in with its surroundings and would never be considered outstanding or unique. The old part of the building, completed in 1910, was constructed to house offices and workspace for the rapidly growing industrial section of Charlotte.

From 1910 until 1952, a janitor by the name of Lonnie Beleran, kept this building spotless. Beleran was a distinguished-looking African American man, who, despite the title janitor, was affectionately called "The Gentleman" by everyone who worked in the building. Lonnie Beleran cleaned, painted, and maintained order in all parts of the building for forty-two years. He could be seen one day mopping a bathroom and caulking a windowpane the next. Despite the cleaning and the dirty mess it often produced, Lonnie Beleran was always pristine. During workdays, he always wore a pure white work suit with neatly polished black, leather shoes.

Lonnie Beleran and the longtime owner of the building were the best of friends, despite living in the pre-civil rights era. The owner also managed the building and he and Beleran saw each other nearly every weekday for over forty years. The two men literally grew old together.

Haunted Charlotte

Things in the office building were mind-numbingly routine; nothing much ever seemed to happen there. The only thing ever noted was a stranger who appeared to be lurking around the back loading dock. After a couple sightings in the summer of 1940, he seemed to disappear without incident. The days were quiet around the building in the years after that.

Then, on the morning of Monday, October 20, 1952, the manager arrived early to open up for business. The building had an eerie sense about it. The manager felt a weird vibe upon approaching the front doors that chilly morning. As the manager turned the key and unlocked the doors, a smell emanated from inside. As he opened the doors and entered, he was almost overwhelmed with horror, a horror that both repelled and attracted him. The manager, a normally steady man, not one to scare easily, began to search the building for the source of the sensations. He started his search in the front foyer and then, office by office, he made his way upstairs. In each area of the building, he encountered a growing sense of uneasiness. His calls of, "Is anyone here?" went unanswered. As the manager opened each door, it creaked on its hinges to reveal an unbothered and unoccupied room. The manager continued through the building, but nothing was out of place—everything seemed normal. After more than thirty minutes of searching, the sense of doom only became stronger.

At last, the manager made his way to the back stairway and stood looking down the long, marble staircase in horror. Starting on the third step down was blood—a lot of blood. It looked as if it had been there for some time, a couple of days maybe. The edges of the blood trail were dried and beginning to crack. The center of the blood was dark and stagnant. The blood trail wandered in irregular splatters down the stairs. With great freight and greater hesitation, the manager began to walk down the large marble staircase. He was careful to sidestep the blood, but when he went to brace himself against the staircase walls, he soon realized the bloodstains were on the walls as well. Step by horrifying step, the manager crept down the stairs. With each step downward, he felt sick to his stomach and it was all he could do to keep from passing out.

As he turned the last corner on the ground floor, there before him was the contorted body of Lonnie Beleran, lying prostrate across the back foyer. The Gentleman janitor's lifeless body was drenched in dried blood. A large flap of flesh was visible dangling down over his neck. Several flies swarmed about the head and hands, happily traipsing through the wounds. His left arm, obviously broken, lay at an awkward angle under the corpse.

It seemed that Lonnie Beleran, on the previous Friday evening, October 17, had stayed late to mop the stairs after everyone else had left for the

5: The Gentleman Janitor

A clean, haunted building; the structure tells no tales.

weekend. The subsequent police investigation revealed that he had slipped on the wet marble and hit his head. The impact with the hard marble stairs had split open his head and he had tumbled down the staircase, leaving a trail of blood behind him. No one will ever know how long it took Lonnie Beleran to die in that stairwell. The police ruled the death an accident.

On the following Wednesday, a funeral was held at the Central Baptist Church with most of the building's employees, including the manager, in attendance. While barely able to contain his sorrow, the manager presented Madge Beleran, Lonnie's widow, with a large bouquet of flowers. Later, at the reception, he presented a check to Madge, a check large enough to establish a college fund for their two grandchildren, Liz and Joshua. Lonnie Beleran was then laid to rest.

Business in the building, however, was never quite the same. The manager, who had liked Beleran as both a friend and an employee, never again felt comfortable in the building. The manager, over the next couple of years, mentioned hearing or seeing Beleran several times and was known to be especially upset over the fact that Beleran's blood had stained the marble stairs and that they had retained a reddish hue. The employees noted that the manager avoided the stairwell, going so far as to walk around the outside of the building to get to the back courtyard area. They listened patiently as the manager wondered aloud about the stranger who had been reported lurking around the building a couple of times a few years back.

The employees had sympathy for the manager, for they too had liked Beleran. They simply marked up to grief the sightings around the rooms. A couple of years later, the manager, unable to cope with the loss of his friend, sold the building to one of the automobile companies.

The building changed hands several times over the next few years, but sightings of Lonnie Beleran continued around the building. The sightings and the rumors were so frequent, in fact, that Lonnie Beleran's name never was lost to history. Various employees and visitors reported seeing a thin man in a clean, white work suit staring at them from around a corner. The reports were too irregular, and from too many people over too much time to be coordinated, and the building began to get a reputation for being haunted. One janitor, who was hired several years after Beleran had died, reported that it was the easiest job he had ever had—that the rooms were always cleaner than he had expected them to be. The janitor said that, on more than one occasion, he found the storeroom stocked when he thought it was low on supplies. On another occasion, a young woman who had come to the building for a job interview later reported that when she was leaving the building after the interview, a pleasant man in a white work suit pointed her to the door. She said she immediately turned around to thank the man for his help, but when she turned, he was gone. The man had simply disappeared without a sound.

No one ever reported that the illusive staring figure attacked him or her in any way. More often than not, the reports stated that the apparition seemed to be oddly comforting and was simply watching over the building.

Taste in décor was changing and, by the 1960s, the long marble staircase was out of style and the newest owners installed trendy yellow shag carpet over the steps. Soon, however, the new carpet began to turn red. Blood red. The employees thought the carpet changing to blood red was creepy and insisted that it be removed. Over time, several other reports of strange occurrences were reported around the building. By the late 1970s, the building was unable to hold an occupant and had become vacant, its glory days behind it.

Without the Gentleman Janitor to maintain it, the building continued to fall into disrepair throughout the early 1980s. It changed hands several times. Soon though, locals began to see something very strange. Not long after it was bought and rehabilitated to its current status, people in the building noticed, even when it was not raining outside, droplets of water would appear on the floor. The roof and plumbing was inspected and no leak was found. In fact, once the drops of water splattered on the concrete,

5: The Gentleman Janitor

they simply vanished. The ghostly figure of Lonnie Beleran was soon seen again, and locals began to claim the drops of water were the tears of the Gentleman Janitor as he mourned for his beloved building.

6
Dr. Narishkeit

The house that once stood on West Graham Street in the 4th Ward district of Charlotte was known as "The house of Dr. Narishkeit." The story begins in 1907, and Dr. Narishkeit was one of the town doctors. He was a general practice doctor and a stout square man of German descent. For several years, he ran his practice out of his home, where he had an office. People from all over town came to see him for complaints ranging from coughs to stomach aches. Occasionally, prospective patients sought him out for things that were more serious, like hallucinations, obsessiveness, and paranormal visions.

By all accounts, he was a competent doctor...but he did have a reputation around town for being a bit odd. The townsfolk thought it strange that he and his son, Ian, never attended church. On occasion, he made people uncomfortable with the things he would say, such as muttering under his breath in German. Although he claimed that his wife had died some years prior, rumors about her sometimes surfaced at society parties.

The practice and the rumors went on for a while without incident, and the townsfolk simply accepted Dr. Narishkeit's...peculiarities. An old wheelchair that sat in his waiting room never sat a living patient, but Dr. Narishkeit would occasionally point to it and remark that if one did not follow his direction, they too, might end up being banished to it. The wheelchair was decrepit even then, and patients were weary of its unseen occupant. Then, in the fall of 1918, things took a slightly darker turn.

A rumor began to circulate that Dr. Narishkeit had been seen one evening in the Old Elmwood Cemetery waving a torch around over one of the tombs, while a tall, slender figure, who seemed to be in a trance, moved

6: Dr. Narishkeit

A photo identified as that of Dr. Narishkeit. It is the only known photo of the Doctor.

slowly around him. After a second sighting in the Old Elmwood Cemetery some days later, the townsfolk began openly speculating that Dr. Narishkeit was practicing standard medicine by sunlight, but Black Magic by moonlight.

Ominously, the rumors and strange sightings went on for a while.

Then, in the fall of 1919, the first in a series of brutal murders occurred in Charlotte, right out on West 4th Street. In fact, the first murder happened while the fullness of the sun still lit the street. It was a horrific murder. A young girl had been sliced up with a knife. She had lost so much blood that her skin was as pallid and grey as a tombstone. The police were, at first, unable to solve the murder that happened near "the house of Dr. Narishkeit." There were simply no clues.

The police opened a full-scale investigation; they combed the town for evidence, searching every alley and watching every cheap bar. Concerned citizens came to the police with tips, but they all turned out to be false leads. The Chief Inspector of the investigation issued a curfew for any woman under the age of twenty-five—they were to be home by 5 p.m. each evening.

Not two weeks into the investigation, another grisly murder occurred in uptown Charlotte. A second girl was found dead a block off North Poplar Street. This girl had her throat slit, nearly decapitating her. She also had several, what appeared to be, razor cuts along the spinal column down her

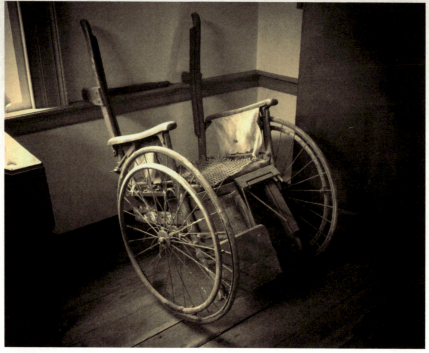

The wheelchair in Dr. Narishkeit's waiting room.

back. The police concluded that the razor marks were made in an attempt to cut off the buttons on her blouse. Her blouse had been removed, but there were no other signs that the crime was sexual in nature. Perhaps, thought the police, the murderer had cut his own hand and bled onto the girl's clothing.

The investigation continued, and the police spared hardly anyone from suspicion. The investigation became, to the townsfolk, almost as oppressive as the lingering threat from a murdering lunatic.

When a third girl was found murdered in the same neighborhood and in a similar fashion, the police department was thrown into a state of chaos. A normally quiet town in the foothills of the Appalachian Mountains, Charlotte now had its first serial murderer. The third crime scene, though strewn with blood, yielded only one usable clue. A shoe print with a blood drop under it was discovered near the sight of the murder. A man by the name of Salvatore Giolitti was brought in for questioning after a woman witnessed him in the area around the time of the murder. He claimed that he had been out that day looking for a new bakery that he had been told had just opened on that side of town. Police demanded he remove his shoes and measurements were made of the soles. The shoes were also inspected for traces of blood, but none was found. While Giolitti waited in a downtown jail cell, comparisons between the shoes and the impressions were made. After several painstaking hours, the report came back. The shoes were a possible match. Had they found their murderer?

The police kept Giolitti in jail and the new developments out of the paper while they investigated further. It was near the end of the second day of the Giolitti investigation that a break came. On the other side of town, an Italian woman named Maria walked into the police station to report her husband missing. She told the police that he had gone out to look for a bakery across town and had never returned. His name was Salvatore Giolitti. The incarceration of Giolitti had been kept a closely guarded secret not to stir the public. The only way Mrs. Giolitti could have known about the bakery story was if it had been the truth. The shoe impression had been a match, but size 9 shoes were very common and hundreds of men in Charlotte wore dress shoes. The police were glad to let an innocent man go, but remained frustrated that they had not been able to catch the crazed killer.

The citizens of Charlotte, on the verge of widespread hysteria, demanded answers. The killings had gone on for three months and only one suspect had actually been taken in for questioning. Christmas was approaching, and no one wanted to have the murders dampen holiday spirits. The newspaper, which had always been supportive of the police, began to print articles casting doubt on the police's ability to be effective. Everyone who had a daughter, wife, or sister was on edge. The police caught a break when the town was quiet and peaceful over the Christmas and New Year holiday season.

But, no sooner had the New Year come than the city of Charlotte was ravaged by yet another murder. A seventeen-year-old girl was found slain in the back of an unattended wagon just a few yards from the corner of West 3rd and Locust Streets. She had been cut open from head to toe, sliced nearly to the bone. She was discovered due to her blood dripping down through the cracks in the wagon's floor and pooling on the street under the wagon. Her ankle was broken in what the police described as an attempt to escape the clutches of her murderer. The murderer eluded capture and no arrests were immediately made.

Four days later, the blouse of the second victim was found down near the docks. The buttons had been cut off and it was soaked in dried blood. The lab analyzed it and found no other useable traces of evidence on the garment. The police could hardly bear the publicity of another dead end.

A few weeks later, a fifth murder darkened the neighborhood around the house of Dr. Narishkeit. This time, however, clues had been left behind. The victim's body was found lying behind some shrubs in the yard of Dr.

Narishkeit. The body had been nearly eviscerated in its now eerily signature manner that was becoming a trademark. As blood soaked into the ground where the body lay, an astute police officer noticed something shiny under the girl's left shoulder. When the police rolled her over, they found a knife under the corpse. The knife was no ordinary kitchen knife; it was a custom knife, of German origin. The inscription, on a brass plate and inlaid into the handle, simply read "Danke SchÖn, Dr. Narishkeit." The knife was immediately taken to the police chief.

The Chief had Dr. Narishkeit brought into the station for questioning that very day. When asked about the knife, Dr. Narishkeit acknowledged that it was indeed his, but that he had dropped it in his yard the day prior to the murder and forgotten about it. He said that he had been using it to cut steaks on his outside patio grill. He said the knife must have simply fallen off the patio and flipped up under the shrubs where the body was left by the real murderer later that night. Dr. Narishkeit's reasoning, to the police, was outlandish, but they had to admit plausible. A few hours later, a comparison report on the knife and the young girl's wounds came into police headquarters. The coroner said the knife might have made the wounds, but might not have. The inconclusive report infuriated the police chief, for as a result, he had to let Dr. Narishkeit go free. Late into the night, the police chief seethed. He told his first deputy that Dr. Narishkeit was now the prime suspect and that they were not to take their eyes off him. Dr. Narishkeit's every move was to be scrutinized. For weeks, the police kept a close watch on Narishkeit's house.

The pressure from the police finally got to Dr. Narishkeit and he went mad. After two officers spent the night on his front porch, Dr. Narishkeit suffered a fit of mania on the steps of his house. When additional police arrived, he shouted profanities at them. He flailed his arms around out of control. His contorted face showed nothing but maniacal contempt for anyone who stepped near him. The town officials seized their opportunity to take Dr. Narishkeit into custody, and they promptly dragged him off to the state insane asylum. If they could not charge him with murder, they were going to have him declared insane; either way, he was going to be locked up for a very long time.

Upon his capture, the neighborhood around Dr. Narishkeit's house fell silent—no more girls were found murdered, and the police believed they had their murderer. Slowly the town began to get back to normal. Eventually, the citizens of Charlotte began to forget…

Then…it happened again. It was the same as before: a girl sliced up with a knife nearly beyond recognition. Once again, the police were unable

6: Dr. Narishkeit

This wall and sidewalk area is, according to legend, the site of one of the murders committed by Dr. Narishkeit.

to solve this murder or either of the two other similar murders that occurred within a week of the newest attacks.

Ian, thought the police. Where was Narishkeit's son, Ian? Had anyone seen him since his father had been locked away? Was Ian the figure in the trance?

The headline in the newspaper the next day read, "Police denied search warrant due to lack of evidence." As the police now had been relegated to a position of incompetence, the townsfolk had had enough of the Narishkeits and a vigilante mob, led by the husband of the first victim, stormed the house and burned it to the ground. The fear and anger of the citizenry simply boiled over. The flames raged into the cloudy night sky until the first cracks of dawn began to appear over the horizon. No one involved in the fire was arrested; in fact, some of the police officers themselves would have done the same thing, save their badges. The next morning when the police searched through the rubble, they found no trace of Ian. They found no corpse, no bones, nothing.

No one knows what ever happened to Ian Narishkeit. Was he killed and consumed in the flames? Did he escape from the fire and run away? Had there ever really been an Ian? No one will ever know; a horrible lingering mystery is all that remains of the house of Dr. Narishkeit.

7
An Amended Sense of Happiness

No two young people could have been more in love than Shana Toberlin and Declan Setter. They met at a spring dance their sophomore year in high school and were inseparable from that time on. While the pressures and influences of high school raged around them, they held tight to each other, although by her own admission, Shana was a bit of a daddy's girl. She saw in her father a man who was strong and wise, both fallible and invincible. Her father, Tom, had always had a soft spot for his only daughter and she had always been able to wrap her dad around her finger. Shana also noticed how her father always treated her mother with love and respect. She saw many of those same qualities in Declan, so the two of them got along as if destiny had introduced them.

Few that knew them were surprised when they chose to attend the same college in the fall of 1954. Shana and Declan fit in well and made many friends quickly. They both had plenty of opportunity to date other people, but they were still madly in love and stayed close as a couple throughout their college years. It seems that education and romance were in the air at the University of North Carolina at Chapel Hill in the mid 1950s, and the next four years passed quickly for the young couple.

7: An Amended Sense of Happiness

The Church.

In the spring of 1958, Shana Toberlin and Declan Setter graduated with honors and moved back to their hometown of Charlotte, North Carolina. Declan had his degree in Business and Shana had hers in Economics. Their future looked bright that spring and almost as soon as their mortarboards hit the ground, Declan and Shana were able to get jobs in their respective fields with local companies.

The next year, the two young lovers began to plan their wedding. Shana spent her free time dress shopping with her mother, while Declan went to see about tuxedo rentals with his father. The couple arranged with their minister, Reverend Samegrelo, to perform the ceremony. Rehearsals began so that all parts of the wedding would run smoothly, with all knowing where to be when the moment was right. Invitations were sent out and the big day was fast approaching.

A couple of days before the big day, Shana attended a wedding shower that was being thrown by her friends. The women exchanged funny gifts and enjoyed each other's company. The men held a bachelor's party for Declan, but no one had really considered him a bachelor since his sophomore year in high school. The guys drank beer and watched the movie *Teenagers from Outer Space*.

Haunted Charlotte

On the day of her wedding, although she had not slept much that night, Shana got up early. Starting at around 7 a.m., Shana, her mother, the bridesmaids, and several friends began to get ready for the 11 a.m. wedding. The women were a flurry of activity. Showers taken and breakfast eaten, the girls began to get dressed, do their hair, and put on makeup. Shana was nervous and excited; she couldn't help dancing around the room to squeals of excitement from the other girls. The women had agreed to meet Mr. Toberlin, Declan, and the other gentlemen at the church. At around 10 o'clock in the morning, Shana, her mother, and three of the bridesmaids left the Toberlin house to go to the church for the wedding.

As the women left the house and got in their car, they laughed and told each other funny stories from the rehearsals. Shana talked about her upcoming honeymoon trip to Paris, France; she had always wanted to visit France and Declan was curious about French architecture. They had settled on France weeks earlier and gotten their passports in order, Shana told the other women. Two of the bridesmaids, Hillary and Laurie, asked Shana questions about France, but mostly about Declan and the wedding. Mrs. Toberlin was driving, while Shana was riding in the front seat, but looking over her shoulder towards the three other women in the backseat. The five women talked and laughed as if they had not a care in the world.

The ride to the church was going along fine when, out of nowhere, a large truck slammed into Mrs. Toberlin's car. The force of the impact crushed in the passenger side of the vehicle and sent it hurling into an enormous marble monument that was in the center of the median. The truck that had hit them spun around and came to rest on the opposing sidewalk against a brick wall. Mrs. Toberlin's car was completely demolished in the accident. Shana and the bridesmaid on the passenger side of the car were killed instantly.

Mrs. Toberlin and the two other bridesmaids were seriously injured, but alive. They were taken to the emergency room at a local hospital downtown. The driver of the truck that had hit the Toberlin's car was declared dead in the ambulance on the way to the hospital. He had received a large cut across his clavicle bone and deep into his neck. The driver bled out within minutes. Word of the accident spread quickly, and a thoughtful police chief sent an officer to the church to inform the other members of the wedding party of the tragedy.

Declan, his father, and Tom, in the meantime, had already gotten to the church. Declan had been excitedly walking up and down the aisle in the sanctuary when word of the accident reached him by way of an in-person visit from the police. He was devastated. Desperate screams of "Nooooo!" could be heard throughout the church building. The other men at the church

7: An Amended Sense of Happiness

reacted with astonishment and incredulity. They, too, were left in a state of panic.

Mrs. Toberlin survived the crash, along with two of the bridesmaids. They survived, but their lives would never be the same again. Shana was buried in the Toberlin family plot at the church graveyard. Mr. and Mrs. Toberlin would grieve for their daughter every day. Mrs. Toberlin even wrote a long letter of mourning to Declan, to express how sorry she was for their mutual loss. Declan spent a year in mourning. He continued to go to work, but did little else.

On the one year anniversary of what would have been Declan and Shana's wedding, something strange happened at the church. Another wedding party was in the reception hall planning for an upcoming wedding, when several of the wedding party members burst through the doors and loudly whispered that they had just seen a ghost in the sanctuary. They were part of the floral committee and they were on a side aisle discussing flower arrangements, when they collectively heard the very distinct sound of a wedding dress train dragging on the floor of the center aisle. When they looked over, they saw the nearly transparent ghostly figure of a young woman in a wedding dress. Instantly, the floral women recognized the apparition as that of Shana Toberlin, the bride who had been killed on her wedding day one year prior. They recognized her due in part to the legend that had sprung up in the community around her death. She was dressed in her magnificent wedding gown and walking slowly down the aisle to get married. What was most strange though, was the fact that the dress was pure white and in perfect repair, as if nothing had happened to her on the way to the wedding. Her face was unmistakable, but she seemed to have a hollow sadness about her that she had never had before.

Declan Setter began bringing flowers to Shana's grave, starting what was to be a lifelong tradition.

Exactly one year later, on the second anniversary of the tragedy, several people again reported seeing the ghostly presence of Shana Toberlin walking down the center aisle of the church wearing her wedding gown. Her nearly translucent figure cast no shadow and made no noise as it silently glided toward the pulpit. Off in the distance, the strange sound of church bells subtly rang out. One woman, upon seeing the apparition, fainted, while another woman remarked on the sorrowful expression held by the ghostly face.

In fact, every year, on the anniversary of the tragedy, Shana's ghost could be seen walking down the aisle of the church. Shana was seen over several years by many people, all of whom reported seeing her in a similar state: translucent and dower. Some who saw the glowing specter of the bride on

The graveyard near the church, rumored to be haunted.

the anniversary of her wedding day also reported seeing the ghostly presence of Shana's bridesmaid, Hillary, alongside her. There were, over the next few years, reports of wailing in the chapel's dressing room.

Then, a few weeks before the twentieth anniversary of the ill-fated wedding, Mr. Toberlin, the bride's father, passed away in his sleep. Mrs. Toberlin was now alone in the world; her last remaining relative had passed on. Declan Setter sat with Mrs. Toberlin at her husband's funeral. A few weeks later, Mrs. Toberlin returned to the church where she was to have become Declan's mother-in-law, a church she had attended regularly all her life. She came to pray on the anniversary of what would have been her daughter's wedding. Upon finishing her prayers, she looked up to see her daughter's ghostly figure walking down the aisle. She had heard rumors of her daughter's ghostly presence, but had never seen it for herself. She gasped as the apparition appeared before her. In amazement, she stared, as not only did her daughter's ghost appear before her, but, suddenly, her husband's, too.

Mrs. Toberlin stood up, barely able to believe what she was seeing. Before her, walking down the aisle, was her daughter being accompanied by her husband. It seemed his ghostly form had returned to walk his daughter down the aisle. Father and daughter, ceremoniously walking together hand in ghostly hand. It was all too much, and Mrs. Toberlin passed out from

7: An Amended Sense of Happiness

fright, only to be revived after some effort on the part of the choir director. Mrs. Toberlin had only a faint recollection of her ghostly vision when she regained consciousness a few minutes later. She spent that night in a restless mood, telling Pastor Samegrelo and the assistant minister about the sighting of her daughter and husband. Mrs. Toberlin was a strong woman and she carried on with dignity and perseverance.

Over the next year, all was quiet and normal in the church; no visions or ghostly apparitions were seen and the members went about their business. On the twenty-first anniversary of the tragedy and the first anniversary of Tom Toberlin's deathly appearance, members of the church reported once again seeing Shana and Mr. Toberlin walking, in ghostly form, down the aisle of the church, as the eerie sound of church bells could be heard in the distance. This year, though, Shana's translucid face bore a reserved uneasy smile. Her father's ashen face, though ghostly, conveyed an amended sense of happiness.

The sightings of Shana and her father continued annually for many more years. The ghostly spirit of Shana, it seemed, was a permanent fixture in the church. Then, just after the forty-sixth anniversary of the wedding day accident, in 2005, Mrs. Toberlin quietly passed away in her bed. Declan Setter, who had remained friends with the Toberlin family, attended the funeral. She, alongside her husband and daughter, was laid to rest in the church graveyard.

The members of the congregation and some townsfolk noted that Declan would bring flowers to the Toberlin grave on the anniversary of both the accident and on the date of Mrs. Toberlin's passing. The flowers he brought were always pure white, and matched the ones that had been in the sanctuary that fateful morning so many years prior.

Eight years later, on Friday, September 13, 2013, Declan Setter passed away. Declan had never married, or even dated, since the untimely demise of his heart's only love. Although he continued to prosper in business and friendships, he never again found true love. He had carried the melancholy of that tragic day with him for the remainder of his life. The Reverend Ferrier said prayers, as Declan Setter was laid to rest in the same graveyard as his beloved Shana.

The fifty-fourth anniversary of the wedding day tragedy came around a few days later on Saturday, September 21, 2013. The church was eerily quiet that day and only a few staff people were around, including Reverend Ferrier. At a few minutes after 11 a.m., curiosity got the best of the Reverend and Mrs. Ferrier and some staff members. They went to look out over the large and well-lit sanctuary. What they saw will likely be whispered about for years to come.

Haunted Charlotte

There before them, they saw as plainly as anything they had ever seen before, floating up the aisle, the ghostly figures of Shana, being escorted by her father, while Declan's haunting presence could clearly be seen waiting for her near the pulpit in the front of the sanctuary. The three of them, in the other ghostly world, were continuing with the wedding while Mrs. Toberlin watched from the pews. As the church staff watched, an unseen minister conducted the wedding. After the saying of the vows, Shana's and Declan's ghosts turned and, hand-in-hand, glided slowly down the aisle toward the vestibule. When they neared the back of the church, the doors flung open without assistance. Shana and Declan moved eerily through the open doors and out into the light. With the wedding of Shana and Declan at last concluded, the couple disappeared into history, never to be seen or heard from again.

8
Mr. & Mrs. Benson

The house along Main Street in Pineville, North Carolina, is for sale and has been for a very long time. The old colonial is not that expensive, but it needs a little work. People in the neighborhood wonder why such a gorgeous old home has not sold. Real estate agents rarely show the extensive property that has been sitting vacant for many years. Oddly, those in the neighborhood have realized that the house never seems to deteriorate or fall prey to vagrants, and yet, they do not know why.

The original part of the house was built in 1830 for the Benson family—Mr. and Mrs. Benson, a newly married couple in their late teens. Upon the exchanging of their vows, the couple moved into the house. Mrs. Benson had inherited a small amount of money from her father, who had recently passed away, and Mr. Benson was a local gunsmith, as was his father before him. Both the elder and younger Benson men were good at the gunsmithing trade.

As the couple settled into the house, they began to establish a daily routine. Mr. Benson would head off each morning to the gunsmith shop just down the street for a day's work making long rifles. Mrs. Benson, planning to be a mother and homemaker, would spend her time getting the house in order for the children she hoped would be coming along soon. The

Haunted Charlotte

The coffin in which Mrs. Benson lay at the funeral parlor…the first time.

couple spent their free time planting a garden and making sure the shed was stocked for the winter months.

Those were happy times for the Benson family; the expectation of parenthood was thrilling for the young couple. They would go to market each Saturday and obtain furniture for what was to be the children's room. Every man in town knew Mr. Benson through the gunsmith shop and every visit would end with some customer cheerfully saying, "Can't wait to see a little Mr. Benson in here." They attended church each week, where Mrs. Benson's friends were all busy making bonnets and blankets for a hopefully upcoming baby shower.

One dreary evening, Mr. Benson came home late from the gunsmith shop, only to find his wife in the kitchen…dead. Her body was sprawled out on the hardwood floor face down. He rolled her over, but her skin was pale and her limbs were lifeless. Mr. Benson was in shock—here a young man and already a widower, and without even yet being a father. After some time he was able to gather himself enough to make his way to his front door, to call out into the street for the doctor. Within minutes, Dr. Collins arrived, pronounced Mrs. Benson dead, and sent an errand boy for the undertaker. Later that night, the undertaker's wagon arrived and took Mrs. Benson's corpse to the mortuary. Mr. Benson rode along in the wagon to

8: Mr. & Mrs. Benson

oversee his wife's placement in her coffin and to arrange a funeral with the director.

Mr. Benson walked home alone through the chilly fog that night, stopping off at the pub to get a bottle of bourbon to drown his sorrow. He drank excessively late into the night, but woke up early the next morning with the thought that he wanted his wife buried in her Sunday best. He washed his hands, went to the family chest, got out Mrs. Benson's long white silk dress, wrapped it neatly in burlap and took it down to the undertaker's place. He presented the dress to the funeral director, asking that it be used for her ceremental garment. It was a reasonable request and he was not denied.

Mr. Benson then wandered back home through the street to his large, empty house, his grief, and a bottle of bourbon. He began to drink away the day and into the night, while the shadows of bereavement encircled his unsober mind. All manner of remorse and reminiscence flashed through his thoughts. He continued to drink past the midnight hour and, at about three in the morning, a drunken sleep began to overtake him. His heavy eyelids began to close and his head began to sink into his folded arms.

Then, just as he fell into a state of unconsciousness, he heard a knock at the door. The weak, but determined, knock persisted for what seemed to him like hours. He finally rose and, in a drunken state, staggered to the door. With much effort, he finally got the door open, only to discover that what stood before him was the ghostly figure of his wife!

"Surely an apparition of my grief!" he said. "Assuredly, it is a specter of my broken heart that stands before me." Mr. Benson rubbed his swollen, drunken eyes. He nearly pulled the wooden door off its hinges in an attempt to remain standing. Still, the illuminated figure of deathly beauty stood before him in the open doorway.

He must have passed out and fallen back into the foyer. Mr. Benson was out cold, from drink, or fright, or a combination of the two. He woke up a couple of hours later tucked neatly in his own bed. Upon awakening, he sat up, wiped his brow, and clutched his chest. The room was lit only by a single candle that was burning low. He could barely believe his eyes; there before him, sitting on the end of his bed, was his wife. *An illusion of my sadness*, he thought to himself. *My memories come back to haunt me*, his still drunken mind beckoned to him. He took his handkerchief to clear his bloodshot eyes, only still to see, at the end of his bed, the lovely figure of his wife. Then, he looked over at his bedside table and there sat a steaming hot cup of tea. *Wait*, he thought. *A spook can do many things, but make tea, I think not.*

He looked back to the end of his bed in disbelief; the figure there was indeed…his wife. She had not died, the doctor later explained, but merely had a fit of catalepsy, a nearly deathlike trance that slows one's breathing and heart rate until even a doctor cannot tell the difference between it and death. To her own overwhelming surprise, she had awakened in her coffin at the mortuary. She had crawled out of her casket and staggered home through the middle of the night's darkness. She had been the one to knock on the door.

Mrs. Benson went on to live for another sixty-three years. She and Mr. Benson eventually raised five children in the house and, for all those years, they laughed about the episode of catalepsy. Mr. Benson, for his part, never drank again. The frightful tale of catalepsy went on to become quite a family story. For decades, the Bensons told and retold the story to their children at Halloween. As she grew older, Mrs. Benson told the story to her many grandchildren when they came to visit.

When Mrs. Benson died a natural death in 1895, she said on her deathbed, "You have taken me for dead once from this house, but you will never take me for dead again!"

Legend has it that real estate agents cannot sell the house because the ghost of Mrs. Benson has never left.

9
Like a Lunatic

When Darrin and Jenny Haubt had twins last year, they bought a larger ranch style house in the suburbs of Mecklenburg County. The house was in a relatively safe neighborhood, although a burglary one block over had made the new parents a bit more cautious. Darrin and Jenny always thought of their children first and nightly security checks were becoming routine. They confirmed that the doors were locked and the garage light was on, in case of a problem. As usual, the family's dog, Shadow, was curled up in her doggie bed near the front door.

One Tuesday night, when everything was deemed quiet, Jenny and Darrin set the automatic alarm system and headed off to bed. It had been a long day, and Darrin was glad to finally pull the covers up and turn out the lights. A soft, restful darkness settled over the Haubts house that night. Darrin fell quickly off to sleep, while Jenny spent a moment to note that the children had settled down without a fuss, and she was grateful for the change of pace. Jenny was soon asleep alongside Darrin.

It was 2:17 a.m. when the calmness was broken by Shadow, who suddenly began barking like a lunatic at the moon. Shadow, usually a heavy sleeper, was barking furiously and running back and forth between the bedrooms and the living room. Both parents and children were awakened by the noise. Darrin, half asleep, grabbed the baseball bat that he kept under his bed and cautiously headed into the hallway. Meanwhile, Jenny grabbed her cell phone and went to the children's room.

Darrin said, "Keep them quiet…if I yell, call the police."

Jenny nodded. Darrin crept into the living room while wondering if the

Haunted Charlotte

Shadow, resting on her bed.

alarm was going to go off. Shadow still paced, although, by this time, she had quit barking. Darrin moved through the house; he looked in all the rooms, but everything was normal. He let out a sigh of relief and went to tell Jenny that everything was fine. The family went back to bed, and eventually back to sleep.

The next night, the prior night's ordeal happened all over again. Once more, Darrin got up to Shadow's incessant barking and searched the house while thinking, "Better safe than sorry." All was again calm. There was, for a second night, no burglar, no alarm, and no threat. Darrin headed back to bed, hoping Shadow's barking was not going to become a routine.

When Shadow began barking and pacing furiously for a third night in a row, Darrin was madder at the dog than scared for his family's safety. He did, though, get his baseball bat and head to the living room to check and make sure everything was secure. Jenny watched, once again, over the children—cell phone at the ready. Everything was secure and peaceful downstairs, and Darrin and Jenny went back to bed.

When, for the fourth night in a row, Shadow began barking and pacing intensely, Darrin and Jenny sat up in bed. Darren said to Jenny in a grumpy manner, "It's your turn; I've been around the house for the last three nights and have seen nothing."

9: Like a Lunatic

Jenny looked out the window over a sleeping neighborhood and reluctantly agreed to search the house. With Shadow at her side, she tiptoed down the hallway toward the stairs.

As Jenny walked into the living room, large glowing marks began to appear on the hardwood floor in front of her. She stopped in her tracks, but the illuminations continued to develop slowly in a strange, irregular pattern around the room. Each spot remained for just a few seconds before vanishing into the darkness. Jenny began screaming like a lunatic at the moon…

10
In The Forest

Rodney and Mack had spent the summer exploring their hometown of Mount Holly, North Carolina. They had met a year earlier at the public library, and although they lived a few miles apart, had become good friends. Both boys were seeking summertime adventure, and they had played along the riverfront and ridden their bikes through the neighborhoods of Belmont and Mount Holly ever since school had ended. The summer had been relatively mild and they had spent several nights camping, both by themselves and with other campers. It was late July 1998, and the two boys decided to go explore the forest around Mount Holly before school began in a few weeks. They wanted to spend this time together, as they would be going to different high schools in the fall and did not know when they would see each other again.

Mack got up early that Saturday morning, and, after some urging from his mother, had breakfast. He packed his book bag with lunch and bottled water, then took off on his bike to meet Rodney. Meanwhile, Rodney was eating breakfast with his mother and father and his younger sister, but paying more attention to the day's exploration than his food. Rodney was running late that day because he had to help his father load the family car to take his sister to camp over in South Carolina. Once the car was packed and his book bag ready, Rodney was free to meet his friend.

10: In The Forest

Mack arrived at the meeting spot first and locked his bike to the fence around back of the convenience store near the edge of the forest. He sat down on the curb to wait for Rodney, who was dropped off at the store by his father a few minutes later. Mack waved enthusiastically at Rodney as the car pulled up to the curb. Mack, naturally polite, came over to the car to say "hi" to Rodney's father and sister. As Rodney's father pulled away, waving into his rearview mirror, the two boys set off into the woods for a day of exploring.

The woods around Mount Holly were extensive, and the two boys had all day to explore. Both Rodney and Mack were in father-and-son camping programs and knew the forest well. They were fourteen, responsible, and had promised their parents that they would be careful, watching where they went.

The two boys hiked together for several hours, quizzing each other on trees, picking flowers, and catching frogs. They found some broken limbs and made a temporary fort. The two boys used sticks as swords, each defending the fort from the other one and, eventually, calling a truce. Over the course of the day, they moved deeper and deeper into the forest, losing track of time and space. The forest became a wonderland in their minds, with all manner of games and fun things to do. As the late August sun filtered through the tree leaves, the boys sat on a log to eat their lunch. Mack had peanut butter and jelly with potato chips, while Rodney brought leftover meatloaf and an apple. Rejuvenated after lunch, the two boys set off once again to explore the forest and its offerings. With trees to climb and creeks to ford, the boys played without regard for the outside world. Rodney and Mack came across a large turtle that they picked up and placed back near the creek so it could get to the water. For several more hours, the boys played and explored the hills somewhere south of the Belmont and Mount Holly neighborhood.

Late in the afternoon, the two exhausted boys sat down for a rest. Rodney asked, "What time is it getting to be?"

"I dunno," Mack answered. Neither boy had remembered to pack a watch.

"It must be getting late; we'd better head back," Rodney said.

"Okay," Mack replied.

The two boys got up from where they were sitting and started to look around.

"Say…" said Mack. "Which way do we go?"

"Well, I think it's this way," Rodney replied, while pointing westward.

Mack looked around, and said to Rodney, "No, I think it's in this direction."

The boys argued for several minutes about which way to head before they both fell quiet, each one looking around, not quite sure where they were or which way was the way out of the forest.

Finally, after several long minutes, Rodney looked at Mack and said, "We're lost." And Mack agreed.

Rodney and Mack started walking, not really knowing where they were going. They agreed to look over the next hill to see if they could get a sense of direction. After more than a half hour of wandering around, the boys began, once again, to quarrel about the direction in which they were headed. Mack wanted to follow the sun west, while Rodney thought they needed to keep the sun to their left and head north. The argument escalated to a real fight, as each boy became more and more frightened. The only thing they could agree on was that they had become completely lost. Rodney complained that Mack was wasting daylight, while Mack complained that Rodney was being stubborn. The two of them sat on a large rock, tired and frightened, and steamed at each other.

It was not long before Rodney looked up and saw before him a softly glowing, yet nearly translucent figure of a young woman. She was stunningly beautiful, with a paisley blanket wrapped around her shoulders. Rodney could clearly see her features, but he could also see the forest through her. He rubbed his eyes. *I must be hallucinating,* he thought. When he looked again, the ghostly woman was still standing before him. As he stared at her, she extended her hand to him, as if to offer assistance or guidance in some way. The ghostly woman spoke in a strange, eerie voice that was both beautiful and hollow. She said to Rodney, "Follow me, and I will guide you out of the forest." She slowly began to turn and move away. Rodney could hardly wrap his mind around what he was seeing and hearing; was this ghostly angel here to save him? Was she there, or just a figment of a tired, frightened mind?

Rodney punched Mack in the shoulder as if to say, "Hey man, we're saved." Mack grumbled something about being lost and for Rodney to leave him alone. Rodney tore his eyes away from the ghostly woman long enough to look over at Mack. He started to plead with him that the woman knew the way out. If they just followed her, they would be out of the woods and back at the convenience store in no time.

Mack looked around the forest and then back at Rodney. He said in an angry voice, "What the hell are you talking about? What woman?"

Rodney pointed to the ghostly woman who was moving away from the two boys and quickly disappearing into the forest.

"You're crazy; you're seeing things," said Mack, as he got up and stormed off in the other direction.

10: In The Forest

In the forest.

Rodney knew in a flash that he had a difficult choice to make. He could follow Mack or follow the ghostly figure that knew the way out of the forest. His head moved back and forth like a tennis match spectator as his mind searched for an answer. If he waited or took the time to convince Mack, the woman would be gone and with her his chance to make it home before sunset. He chose to follow the ghostly woman.

Rodney lost all thought of Mack as he ran after the ghostly figure that was rapidly getting ahead of him. He ran and ran, following her radiating trail through the forest. Soon, the trees began to thin and Rodney found himself at the edge of the forest. He crouched in exhaustion, putting his hands on his knees and lowering his head to exhale. When he stood up a moment later, the ghostly woman was gone. Rodney looked around, desperate to locate her. No sooner did he begin to panic, than the convenience store came clearly into view. Rodney ran to the store as fast as he could. As he came around the back fence he saw Mack's bike still sitting there locked to it. Rodney quickly turned around to see his father pulling into the parking lot to pick him up.

"Hi son!" Rodney's father shouted through the car window.

Rodney ran up to his father in the car and immediately started to tell the story of getting lost and the ghostly woman and leaving Mack and….

"Stop," said Rodney's father. "Slow down and tell me what happened," his father said with a worried look on his face.

Rodney told his father the whole story of the day's events. "We've got to find Mack!" Rodney said, ending his pleas nearly in tears.

Rodney's father called the Mount Holly police and a search was soon underway. A dozen police officers and volunteers quickly began searching the woods near the store. Two hours later, as dusk was creeping along the horizon, a police radio dispatcher announced that Mack had been found. He was scared and hungry, but otherwise well.

Meanwhile, during the search, a police officer made a report about the incident. While interviewing Rodney and his father, the officer mentioned that a few years prior, a young girl named Estella had gone missing in those same woods, but she had never been found. A police officer came by to get Mack's bike while another officer took him home. Mack was understandably mad at Rodney for leaving him in the woods, although he did admit that he had been the one to storm off into the forest. Rodney's father was glad that both boys were safe at the end of the day. He took Rodney home for a bath and a hot meal. Rodney felt bad about how the day had ended. To both boys' regret, they never saw each other again after that.

By the spring of 2008, Rodney was twenty-four and had become a manager at one of the large factories in the Mount Holly area. That same year he married Janet, his longtime girlfriend. The newly married couple began to plan their future. They bought a new house in a new subdivision just south of Mount Holly. The house was so new in fact, that construction was still going on in the neighborhood when Rodney and Janet moved in. The couple spent their first few days in the house discussing how to arrange the furniture and what color the curtains should be. Rodney planted a couple of maple trees and Janet set out window boxes with fresh flowers. After some decorating and several nights in the house, it began to feel more like their own home.

Then, Rodney, not two weeks after moving into the house, was overcome by a strong sense of fear and anxiety. The terror grabbed him so strongly that he fell to the floor and curled up into a ball. Janet tried to help him to his feet, but he remained on the floor for some time. He did not sleep that night; he just paced in front of the fireplace.

As the days and nights after that stretched into weeks, Rodney kept having panic attacks. Soon, he was claiming to see things. He told Janet that he was being tormented by a sinister figure that was out to take his sanity. He claimed that cobwebs were developing in the kitchen and that he could smell rotting flesh in the spare bedroom. At first, Janet thought it was just stress from work or the new house. She tried her best to be supportive

10: In The Forest

of her husband, but he was beginning to claim that the new house was haunted. He could, he claimed, see spirits in the windows. She told Rodney that she did not believe in ghosts or haunted houses. She wanted to be helpful, but this talk of haunted houses and ghosts was getting to be too much. For the first time in their marriage, Rodney and Janet quarreled.

The argument upset Janet. *How silly,* she thought, *to be arguing over the existence of ghosts.*

"Rodney," Janet argued, "this house is brand new. It couldn't be haunted; only old houses are haunted. Everyone knows that." Janet continued, "Why, just a year and a half ago this whole subdivision didn't even exist. Until then, it was just a forest, unclaimed county land…that's all. How could it be haunted?"

"Forest…what forest?" Rodney asked Janet. "I don't know the name of it. It was behind the old convenience store that used to be just down the road from here."

Forest, thought Rodney…*could it be?* Rodney's mind flooded with memories of that day with Mack, making him feel sick to his stomach. He went to the computer and looked up a map of Gaston County. Sure enough, the subdivision had been built on the site of the forest where he and Mack had played that day years earlier. On the site where that ghostly woman had led him… home.

Janet said she remembered him telling her a story about a day in the forest with a friend, but could not recall the part about a ghost. Rodney retold the story to Janet, but decided not to describe her in any detail; he did not want Janet to think it was all just some teenaged boy's fantasy girl. Rodney and Janet talked about the day in the forest and the terrors he was currently experiencing for several hours, after which Rodney felt better. The couple still disagreed about the existence of ghosts, but Rodney and the house remained quiet and that was fine by Janet.

After an evening walk around the neighborhood a few days later, Janet came screaming into the house. She looked at Rodney with wide-open vacant eyes. She told Rodney, with a shaky voice, that she had just seen a beautiful, but ghostly, woman wearing a paisley blanket over her shoulders.

Rodney quietly said, "Her name is Estella."

11
A Stroll Around the Neighborhood

When he stepped out onto his front porch to get the newspaper and have a smoke, Mr. Tolson noticed that the air was crisp and the new fallen snow set off nicely against the bare branches of the maple trees. He looked first for the newspaper, but it had not arrived yet. He then lit his cigarette and took his first drag of the morning. In looking out over his neighborhood, he could see Charlotte and part of the bend in the hills—a view he had admired from that porch for more than fifty years. Mr. Tolson had grown up in the house where he now stood; he was proud of the fact he knew no other place as home.

The year was 1913, and Mr. Tolson was especially anxious to get the newspaper that morning. He was following the mysterious case of the Voynich Manuscript, and he wanted the latest news. The newspaper boy was usually on time, but the newspaper was not in its usual spot that morning. As he stood on his porch, a couple walked by and he waved at them pleasantly. Oddly, they did not respond. He thought to himself, *They must not have seen me in their haste to get out of the chilly wind.* Mr. Tolson thought to himself that he did not mind the cold; in fact, he rather liked it. Upon finishing his

11: A Stroll Around the Neighborhood

The 4th Ward residential neighborhood as it is today.

cigarette, Mr. Tolson thought he would take a stroll around the neighborhood. Surely, he thought, when I return, I will come home to my newspaper. He stepped back inside the house just long enough to get his coat and hat and tell his wife that he would return shortly.

His wife looked up from her sewing when she heard her husband's voice. She replied, "I'll miss you dear," before returning to her stitching. The butler, who was in the back parlor, raised his head in acknowledgment of Tolson's exchange with his wife. A sly grin came over the butler's face, as if he knew some grave secret.

Mr. Tolson took off around the corner and proceeded to walk toward the park. For what time he was visible, the butler watched him as he strolled along. The air was stiff, but the park was close to home and Mr. Tolson enjoyed taking leisurely strolls there upon occasion. As he walked along, he noticed his neighbor sweeping snow off her front porch. He waved at her, but her head was covered tightly in a shawl and she could not see Mr. Tolson from her porch. She did not wave back to him. He continued on his walk while listening to the church bell ring 8 a.m. Upon passing another neighbor, Mr. Tolson again waved. Again, there was no response from the neighbor, and Mr. Tolson began to think this was all somewhat strange. *Were people just too concerned with the cold to notice me as I walk along?* he thought to himself. *Oh, well. People these days just aren't as friendly as they used to be back in my day.* As he continued to walk toward the park, the wind picked up a bit and it started to blow snow around in swirls of winter beauty. Despite no response from his neighbors, Mr. Tolson was enjoying his walk and, by the time he made it to the park a few minutes later, it was warming up some. He liked a large bench in the park and he decided to sit and watch the people play that day. The warmth of the winter sun had melted the snow by the time he made it to his bench and it was dry. He sat down and breathed in the cold dry air, exhaling a contented and happy sigh. With another cigarette lit, he leaned back to watch the world go by.

There were children and adults playing all around him, some with sleds and some with picnic baskets full of wonderful smelling breads. Mr. Tolson was a bit surprised at how active the park was, given that the temperatures were barely above freezing.

Soon, two children came and sat down on the bench next to Mr. Tolson. They each had toys and seemed oblivious to his presence. As the parents of the two children approached the bench, Mr. Tolson thought, *Finally, someone to talk with.* The adults, though, just sat on the bench and ignored Mr. Tolson when he said "hi." He thought this very strange, but, not being a rude or pushy man, decided it was their prerogative not to talk to someone if they did not want to. He simply looked the other way.

It was not long before Mr. Tolson looked down the sidewalk and recognized the man walking toward him; it was John Kepper, the manager of the docks. He had known John for years. As John approached the bench, Mr. Tolson extended his arm to shake hands with John. Mr. Kepper simply walked on past the bench without so much as a handshake or a hello. Mr. Kepper never turned his head.

This was quite enough; what was this all about anyway? John Kepper, of all people, was not a rude man, but his behavior today deserved an explanation. Mr. Tolson was going to get an answer from John Kepper. No sooner had Mr. Tolson stood up from the bench to pursue John Kepper, than he saw before him Mrs. Jackson, the principal of Evansville's largest school. She had been a teacher when his children were going there; surely, she would talk to him.

"Hello, Mrs. Jackson," Mr. Tolson said when he was within earshot of her. The woman pulled her scarf from around her face as if to respond to Mr. Tolson, only to reveal the soft features of a much younger woman. She whisked on past Mr. Tolson without a care in the world. By that time, John Kepper had disappeared into the crowd.

11: A Stroll Around the Neighborhood

Mr. Tolson spun around on the sidewalk at a pace that almost allowed him to keep up with his spinning mind. What was going on? Why was he being ignored? Did no one recognize him?

He started to walk back home while thinking to himself, *Maybe I'm dreaming… That must be it, some half-awake pre-breakfast delusion. I'll go home and get a hot cup of coffee and some eggs. I'll feel better with a full stomach.* He started back towards home.

Not long after he set off for home, Mr. Tolson came across a beggar in the street. He pulled a quarter dollar from his coat and handed it to the man in the street. The man reached out toward Mr. Tolson's outstretched hand, only to stop just short of reaching the coin. He instead bent his hand upward and made a refusal motion. Mr. Tolson recoiled in disgust. Really…a beggar refusing his coin…what gratitude. Mr. Tolson began to walk off from where the bum sat, and then, out of embarrassment mostly, he turned to look back at the beggar. A surreal scene played out before him. The bum still had his arm extended; he was waving at another person who was across the way. Mr. Tolson fell into a state of confusion. Had the bum been refusing his offering or waving past him?

For the first time on his walk, Mr. Tolson felt a frigid chill come creeping around his neck. He pulled up his coat collar and turned to face the headwinds howling around him. Step after step, Mr. Tolson made his way out of the park. As he reached the street, he grasped the park gate and hung on, nearly fainting. He did not understand what was happening to him; he could not figure out how everything had gotten so weird.

"Hello!" he called out to the man coming down the sidewalk. "Please help me; I feel faint."

The man reached up under Mr. Tolson's arm and took a firm grip, supporting Mr. Tolson. Once Mr. Tolson was sure the man had him steadied, he let go of the gate. Mr. Tolson looked over at the man who was smiling kindly at him.

Nearly crying, Mr. Tolson explained to the man that he had come out for a walk in his neighborhood, but no one had recognized him. He tried to convey to the man that this had made him feel strange, as if he somehow did not exist. At length he rambled on, but soon caught himself and apologized. "Forgive me sir, for I have spoken of my troubles to you, as if we were long-lost friends, when we in fact are strangers." Mr. Tolson continued, "I have been rude, laying all my troubles on you without even asking you your name."

The man replied with only a gentle, knowing smile.

The two men walked along the street with each other, as if they were brothers who had known each other all their lives. Mr. Tolson spoke of his

A view of the neighborhood from Mr. Tolson's house.

impressive business accomplishments, how he was able to take his father's business and dramatically improve on it. Over the course of several blocks, he spoke of weather and politics, nature, and the country's newest invention called an automobile. The man helping him was quiet and reserved, but despite this, Mr. Tolson was comfortable with him and lengthy explanations seemed unnecessary.

The two men stopped into a corner café and had breakfast and coffee. The man with Mr. Tolson sat silently, but somehow Mr. Tolson knew this time that it was all right; he was with whom he needed to be. After both men had eaten toast and eggs, they left the café and continued to walk back to Mr. Tolson's house.

As they walked along, an older couple came up to them. The two men vigorously shook each other's hand and silently greeted one another while Mr. Tolson watched. The man with Mr. Tolson tipped his hat to the woman accompanying the other man, gently kissing her hand. With pleasantries respected, the man turned to Mr. Tolson to introduce him with a wave of the hand.

11: A Stroll Around the Neighborhood

"Welcome to Charlotte," said Mr. Tolson. The other man simply tipped his hat to Mr. Tolson, while the woman bowed her head politely. The other couple seemed to disappear as quickly as they had appeared.

As soon as the other couple was out of sight, Mr. Tolson remarked to the man that he felt much better having met someone who acknowledged his existence. He said he did not know what had happened to him that morning, but that he felt now like his old self again.

Upon arriving back at his house, Mr. Tolson thanked the man for helping him. Mr. Tolson looked the man in the eye and asked, "Will I see you again?"

The man nodded his head as if to say, "I am certain you will," and with that Mr. Tolson turned and walked up the walkway to his house.

The newspaper was waiting for him on his front step. He picked it up, put it under his arm, and turned to wave goodbye to the man who had helped him home. The man was gone; he had completely vanished into the morning's cold wind.

He went into his house and called out to his wife. She did not immediately answer, but that was not unusual; the house was large and he had a soft voice. Mr. Tolson put the newspaper down and hung up his hat and coat. He again called out to his wife and again there was no reply. Room by room, Mr. Tolson searched the house for his wife. *Surely she must be home* he thought, *she would have left me a note if she were going out.*

As he walked into the children's now-vacant room, Mr. Tolson saw his wife sitting on the end of the bed beside her sewing project, sobbing. He was shocked at her condition, and quickly walked across the room to comfort her. As he approached, she got up from the bed and walked out of the room right past him. Mr. Tolson stood in awe at the fact his obviously upset wife had completely ignored him. *She must be upset at me for being so late getting back from my walk*, he thought to himself, as he pursued his wife down the hallway. The butler peered out from around the kitchen door just as Mrs. Tolson passed by its entranceway. The butler quickly closed the door, to remain anonymous to her attention. As he walked behind his wife, Mr. Tolson called out to her with profuse apologies, but she did not respond; she simply kept walking down the stairs and into the front hall.

As Mrs. Tolson walked into the front parlor, she brushed against the newspaper on the front table. It fell onto the foyer floor open to the front page. She cried out, "Where did this damn newspaper come from?"

The butler replied from the other end of the hallway, "I brought it in Mrs. Tolson."

At that moment, Mr. Tolson glanced first at the butler, then down at the newspaper's headline, which read: "John Tolson, local businessman, found murdered! Police baffled."

12
Homeward Bound

Debbie and Ralph Collettini had told themselves that on their 15-year anniversary, they would take a vacation. Ralph worked for his father as a woodworker and Debbie was a nurse at one of the local hospitals. Money was tight, but the Collettinis had always seen themselves as part of the American middle-class dream, and taking a vacation was part of that dream. The twins, Daniel and Frank, were eleven, and little Lynn was almost nine. The Collettinis thought that it was time for them to see somewhere other than Charlotte. For weeks beforehand, they poured over maps and travel brochures, imagining themselves in different places. Debbie asked all her friends about their vacations: where they had been and what they had done. Being a woodworker, Ralph wanted to get a look at the trees wherever they went. They wanted to see America, stretch out and go northwest. Small towns and big cities fascinated them both and neither one of them had been to the Midwest.

After careful consideration, the Collettinis decided on a road trip along the Ohio River, from their hometown of Charlotte to the city of Cincinnati. Debbie's father was from Ohio, but Debbie had never seen it for herself. The Collettinis decided to rent a car for the trip so they could fly home, an experience they wanted the children to have. It would be a great opportunity

12: Homeward Bound

to see several states, and so, they set the date of the vacation to correspond with their anniversary.

The day of the vacation finally came around and, with car packed and children aboard, the Collettinis headed out to see America. Jim and Sala, Ralph's older brother and sister-in-law who lived a few doors down the block, had agreed to feed the dogs and watch the house while they were gone and the senior Collettinis waved them off down the street.

The first day was an adventure, with the children getting restless on cue and traffic causing the usual headaches. Soon though, the bumpy start began to smooth out as the family settled into the trip. The Collettinis made several short stops to look through antique shops as they headed along interstate 40 through Asheville, but their first extended stop was at the Daniel Boone National Forest, on the second day of the trip.

Ralph wanted to appreciate the selection of trees and the children needed to get out of the car and run around for a time. The family parked their car, changed shoes, and started down one of the trails. No sooner were they in the woods than Daniel and Frank started to play hide-and-seek among the trees. Debbie tried to keep the boys contained, while also watching out for little Lynn. Ralph, usually an attentive father, was a bit distracted by the trees on this particular outing. As the family walked along the trails, they each found their own things of interest. Lynn started looking for butterflies, while her mother looked for birds and other small wildlife critters. The twins continued to play robustly along the trail, reluctantly staying near their parents.

Noontime rolled around and the family stopped for lunch at one of the picnic tables, where Debbie spread out a tablecloth and the food. The whole family sat down to eat. Ten minutes later, a man dressed in hiking clothes walked by the Collettinis as they ate their lunch. The man waved pleasantly and Daniel and Frank responded with a wave of their own.

The man said "Fine day for a picnic; you all have fun today."

The twins nodded and said, "You too," in unison.

Ralph looked up from his sandwich and said to the twins, "Who are you talking to?" The boys just giggled at their father, while Debbie shrugged her shoulders and remarked that the incident was strange.

The afternoon passed uneventfully and, as evening approached, the family set off to find a hotel for the night. The hotel was pleasant enough, but Ralph did not sleep well; he had several nightmares before finally getting up around sunrise. Bad dreams were unusual for Ralph, but vacations could be stressful and he and Debbie gave it no more thought.

The next morning, the family repacked the car and headed toward the town of Berea—the arts and crafts capital of Kentucky—to visit local artists and absorb some of the culture. At a gas stop near Berea's town limits, Ralph noticed that Frank and Daniel were making faces out the window. He turned to see who they were looking at, but saw no one. Ralph shook his head at the boys' behavior.

Next, they headed to the Kentucky Horse Park, just north of Lexington. Though it was a sunny day, a cloud seemed to follow Ralph around. He could not escape the sense of strangeness that had come over him. Even Debbie noticed that his demeanor had grown more serious.

The children, though, had a wonderful time playing at the park, watching the horses, and learning how a large farm worked. The Collettini children had been raised in Charlotte, and they had never seen a working horse park before. The children were still full of energy by mid-afternoon, but Ralph was getting tired due to his lack of sleep the night before. While the children played, Ralph and Debbie sat on a bench and talked about the adventures they had been having on the vacation so far. Ralph mentioned how glad he was that they had a reservation the next night at a bed and breakfast. He was looking forward to some quiet time without the children. Debbie, too, expressed how much fun a romantic evening might be. Ralph and Debbie finally relaxed and enjoyed the rest of the afternoon at the Kentucky Horse Park. By early evening, the Collettinis left the Horse Park, got some dinner, and headed to a hotel to get a good night's sleep. The next morning the Collettinis moved on to Cincinnati.

They all arrived in Cincinnati an hour later and had the whole day to explore the city before going to the B&B that evening. The whole family walked around the City of Seven Hills, but as they did, Ralph began to be overcome by that now all-too-familiar strangeness. Debbie, too, began to feel an odd sensation and confided in Ralph that she felt as if she were being followed. It was a creepy feeling Debbie had never experienced before. What should have been a wonderful, happy day on their vacation became for both Debbie and Ralph an exercise in mystifying visions. By late afternoon, the sun was beginning to set and, everywhere Ralph looked, he saw things in the twilight that he was scarcely sure were real. The boys were their usual selves, hungry and exaggerated in mood.

The Collettinis went out for dinner at a local restaurant on the outskirts of Cincinnati. Things were moving along fine for the family, when all of a sudden, the twins started to wave furiously at someone across the restaurant. Ralph strained his neck to see who the boys were waving at, but he could see no one—just a dark empty corner of the dining room. He tapped Debbie on the shoulder and pointed in the direction that the boys were waving. Debbie just looked at Ralph in confusion. Were the twins waving at a waiter, or someone they recognized, or someone or something else? Ralph then

12: Homeward Bound

The Bed & Breakfast in Cincinnati is a grand and haunted home.

looked over at little Lynn; who was just staring off into space as if she had been possessed. Ralph thought to himself, *I'm tired; I'm reading too much into this. Little boys sometimes do unexplainable things.*

Ralph had been hoping to arrive at the Cincinnati Bed and Breakfast, put the children in their room, and enjoy a quiet romantic evening with Debbie, but that was not to be. By the time they arrived, he was exhausted and a little unnerved at the creepy episode with the children in the restaurant. The hostess opened the front door and welcomed them in. She appeared to be a strong woman in her mid-fifties. Debbie noticed right away that the woman had a sense of resigned sadness about her. As the woman started to shut the door, she paused and looked around. Debbie got the feeling that the woman was looking for someone, perhaps another guest. For their part, the children were loaded for bear, full of tired energy and relentlessly running around the large Victorian home. The hostess at the bed and breakfast, Mrs. Lintain, took the children's ebullience in stride; she had seen many tired, but wound-up, children in her thirteen years as a bed and breakfast owner. With patience and fortitude, she helped the Collettinis bring in their luggage and settle in their rooms. Mrs. Lintain handed Debbie the room key and remarked that there would be wine, juice, and snacks available in the living room downstairs and that they were welcome to come down and sit.

With the twins playing in another part of the house and Lynn in her room, Ralph and Debbie unpacked and then decided that some time to relax in the living room sounded like a good idea. The couple went downstairs and Ralph poured both of them a glass of wine. They sat in the large comfortable chairs and bantered about the day. Soon, Mrs. Lintain popped in and asked if there was anything else she could bring them.

"Thank you, we're fine," replied Debbie.

Mrs. Lintain smiled at Debbie and said, "All right then; you all make yourselves at home and I'll see you in the morning."

Debbie noted that Mrs. Lintain had a subtle, yet odd, joy about her—a disposition in stark contrast to the one she had earlier. She wanted to ask Mrs. Lintain if she was all right, but she stopped herself, realizing that Mrs. Lintain was a stranger, no matter how comfortable she made her feel. With that, Mrs. Lintain disappeared into the private section of the house.

Debbie and Ralph drank wine and talked for another thirty minutes, stopping only long enough to note that the children were unusually quiet. A little after nine, they decided that, pleasant though this was, they needed to round up the twins and Lynn and get them to bed. The Collettinis went looking for the boys.

12: Homeward Bound

They searched first the living room, knowing that little boys like to sneak around, and just because they had not seen them, did not mean they were not there. They had no luck finding the twins in the living room, and so continued the search down the hall and into the dining room. The house at first seemed formidable, but the couple kept looking. Unfamiliar shadows passed over the Collettinis as they searched, half expecting the guys to jump out from behind a piece of furniture and try to scare them. The laundry room door squeaked on its hinges as Debbie pushed it open. Only laundry and some old books occupied the room. The kitchen, they thought; the twins sure like to eat. Maybe they went to get a late night snack. The kitchen was dark and empty when Ralph and Debbie entered. The two of them just stood there, letting their eyes adjust to the darkness. *What a beautiful, eerie kitchen*, thought Debbie, as the moonlight began to reveal her surroundings.

All of a sudden, Ralph shrieked and spun around, nearly knocking Debbie over. She grabbed his arm and, nearly shouting, said, "What?"

Ralph bent over and grabbed his chest, clenching his fingers tightly to the fabric of his shirt. His face was contorted in pain; his head swirled in frantic confusion. He glanced up, quickly peering out into the darkness of the hallway. Once he had composed himself, he told Debbie he had seen a moving figure in the highly polished faucet.

No sooner had he spoken, than Mrs. Lintain appeared out of the darkness and came into the kitchen carrying a lamp. It took a moment for the Collettinis to regain themselves. Ralph, already exhausted, shrank into a chair at the kitchen table. Mrs. Lintain put the lamp down while Debbie sat next to Ralph.

Mrs. Lintain apologized, stating that she had heard a noise, and while noises in the bed and breakfast were not unusual, this noise had aroused her, and her curiosity. She offered to make them tea or to warm some milk and Ralph accepted the offer. He began telling Mrs. Lintain about the search for the still-missing children, explaining that was why they had come into the kitchen in the first place. Mrs. Lintain sat down at the large kitchen table to continue their conversation over warm milk and some leftover pound cake.

The three adults sat at the kitchen table like long lost friends and conversed about all manner of things. Debbie wanted to know about Mrs. Lintain's pottery collection and Mrs. Lintain wanted to know what it was like having twin boys. After a few minutes of talking, Debbie felt comfortable enough with Mrs. Lintain to ask her about the change in mood she had displayed earlier in the evening. She started cautiously, not wanting to offend her hostess.

Haunted Charlotte

Mrs. Lintain seemed perfectly willing to talk about it, and so Debbie listened. Mrs. Lintain started by sharing how adroit she thought Debbie's sense of perception was in this regard. Rarely did guests even notice such subtle facial expressions. Mrs. Lintain continued by sharing that thirteen and a half years prior, her husband George had disappeared while hiking in Daniel Boone National Forest.

Ralph abruptly interrupted her, "Daniel Boone National Forest, did you say? We were just there yesterday! My sons, while we were there, saw"…

Debbie cut him off, "Ralph, don't be rude, let her finish."

Mrs. Lintain smiled knowingly, and continued. "I have carried around with me all these years the sadness of his loss; you see, his body was never found. It may sound odd," Mrs. Lintain continued, "but whenever I open the front door, I always look to see if perhaps George has finally made his way home. I guess the thing you picked up on was my sadness at his not being in the doorway. I know it is your anniversary weekend and I guess anniversaries make me miss George just a little more than usual. In fact, I started the bed and breakfast so the house would not be empty, but after you all had arrived tonight, suddenly the house felt different…somehow alive and happy again. I was sitting in my room a few minutes ago, and I did not feel the least bit lonely; in fact, I felt like George—"

At that moment, Daniel and Frank burst into the kitchen shouting, "Mommy, we saw that man again! The one we saw in the woods in Kentucky and again at dinner! He's in the back bedroom right now!" said Frank with excitement.

"Yeah," added Daniel, "He offered to show us his train set; he's here, and he's here right now!"

Debbie turned to look at Mrs. Lintain. She just smiled lovingly at the twins and said, "I know."

13

A Relentless Spinning

Mrs. Whitewell and her two children were running late for church that Sunday morning. However, that was not unusual. What was different that Sunday morning was that the Whitewell family was sponsoring the guest minister, Dr. Whirl. An old family friend, Dr. Whirl was the guest of honor. He and his wife, Mrs. Whirl, had flown in from Japan specifically for the occasion. Mr. Whitewell had left his home early that morning to pick the Whirls up at the airport. The flight from Japan had been delayed in LAX, and Mr. Whitewell and the Whirls went straight to the church that morning. As the call to worship was beginning, Mrs. Whitewell slipped in to the back of the sanctuary and took a seat near Mr. and Mrs. Dearling. She first looked up front to see her husband sitting in the front row watching the services. Then, she looked up toward the dais and saw Dr. and Mrs. Whirl sitting in the service leader's seats, waiting for their introduction.

At the conclusion of the introduction, Mrs. Whirl got up to speak to the large congregation. She gave a few remarks to frame the sermon her husband was about to deliver. The Whirls had the whole congregation's attention. After Mrs. Whirl spoke, Dr. Whirl came to the pulpit and delivered a thoughtful and inspiring sermon. He spoke for more than twenty minutes without a script or a lackluster moment. Dr. Whirl was known throughout Christendom as a scholar and orator of high regard. He had made a career

Local legend says that this is the Church where Mrs. Whirl spoke; then again, local legend says a lot of things.

out of delivering dynamic sermons, and today was no exception. At the conclusion of the sermon, the congregation gave a thundering applause. The choir sang a couple of hymns that corresponded with the sermon and, in just over an hour, the service ended in tears of joy.

The congregation all stood up and flooded the aisles at once, blocking Mrs. Whitewell's path to the front of the sanctuary. She nervously looked around for a way to meet up with her husband and the Whirls. Eventually, she decided that this course of action was foolish; she had shopping and preparations for dinner waiting for her at the house. She would just have to wait to see her husband and the Whirls at dinner. The Whirls, the regular minister, an assistant, and Mr. Whitewell would have lots to do at the church before they all came to the Whitewells' house for an extended family dinner. Mrs. Whitewell gathered up her children, Allison and Corman, and headed out to the car to go grocery shopping.

For the next hour and a half, Mrs. Whitewell shopped for groceries, carefully selecting dinner items to suit everyone's personal menu. With the children in tow, she picked out the freshest fruit, the finest wine, and the best cuts of meat. She had a somewhat tight budget for the occasion, but

13: A Relentless Spinning

the filet mignon was a spare-no-expense item. Spices, bread, and ice cream were also added to the cart to round out the shopping. When she finally got Corman to stop blocking the doorway, they were on their way back to the house for several frantic hours of cooking and cleaning. She was glad she had hired a maid for the day to help her with the chores at hand.

Against her better judgment, Mrs. Whitewell assigned each child a task. She also held no hope that the tasks would be completed correctly or on time. She and the maid went about their preparations methodically and ardently. She was tired, but today was a day of celebrations and an early night was not in the cards. Allison at length came into the kitchen and stated emphatically that the table was set. When her mother checked on the settings, she was overjoyed to find the table correctly set for the eight expected guests. She heaped genuine praise on her daughter and sent her off to play video games in her room. At five minutes of six in the evening, everything was done. The dinner was staged and ready to be served. At six o'clock sharp, Mr. Whitewell and the guests arrived.

Mrs. Whitewell stood dressed and waiting. The maid opened the door as the people arrived, and in walked Mr. Whitewell, Mrs. Whirl, the minister, and his assistant. The maid gathered the guests' coats and hats, taking them to the coat closet. Although everyone had met previously, Mr. Whitewell made a polite round of introductions.

At the end of the introductions, Mrs. Whitewell looked at the guests with a puzzled look on her face. She apologized for not meeting them earlier in the day. Then, with some hesitation, she asked Mrs. Whirl where Dr. Whirl was. "Will he be joining us for dinner?" she asked. "I bought his favorite cut, a filet mignon." She looked into her eyes for an answer, only to see Mrs. Whirl's eyes overcome with sadness.

Mrs. Whitewell looked at the regular minister in confusion. "Did I say something wrong? What's going on?"

A cold chill seemed to descend on the group as they stood in the foyer.

The minister just stared at Mrs. Whitewell for a moment in disbelief, "Have you not heard; did you not know?" the minister replied, with a confused look on his face. He looked over at Mr. Whitewell, who shrugged his shoulders, obviously embarrassed and uncomfortable.

Mrs. Whirl, at long last replied, "My husband died two years ago and was buried in the graveyard at our home church in Indianapolis."

Mrs. Whitewell awkwardly replied, "But…I saw him at church just this morning. He…he was sitting with you on the dais. He delivered a wonderful sermon." Mrs. Whitewell's thoughts began to race through her memories. She continued, "I…I bought filet mignon especially for him; I don't understand…I saw him today." Mrs. Whitewell looked more and more confused. She felt the blood begin to drain out of her face as she continued, "I swear I saw him deliver a sermon at the church this morning…He was wearing a black blazer with small silver buttons, a black and silver paisley tie. His shirt was white, with a short collar. I noticed he had cut his usual beard down to a goatee. I…know I have not seen him in a while before today…but today…I…."

Mrs. Whirl reached out, put her hand on Mrs. Whitewell's shoulder, and said, "Dear, he was buried just as you described."

Mrs. Whitewell, face completely pallid, fainted.

14
Clock & Watch

From the time he had been a young boy, James Barren had been business minded. His father, an accountant and manager, had been a stickler for precision, order, and a well-negotiated deal. The business lessons James's father had instilled in his son were not lost on the young boy. In addition to business, James Barren had always loved scales and watches, especially antique or specialty clocks. One might have argued that the only thing young James loved more than business was measurement devices for things or time. While he appreciated his father's skills with the books, James had always been somewhat more mechanically minded and continued to pursue his fascination with timekeeping and instruments of measurement. When James's father passed away in 1924, James inherited his father's estate and was free to do as he pleased.

In 1925, James Barren opened Barren's Clock & Watch in uptown Charlotte, North Carolina. He traveled around the mid-south. buying old grandfather clocks and antique scales from estate sales and barn buys. He stocked the large shop with every type of clock, from the smallest pocketwatches to the grandest mantle clocks. He had tables made from the finest wood— tables made just for displaying specialty clocks or scales. The brick walls of the shop were lined with every variety of hanging clock one could imagine. Near the center rear of the shop, he put his oversized mahogany desk. At the corner of the desk, he placed a large bronze statue of Lady Justice, with her scales of judgment, for all to see. Over the next thirty years, James gained a reputation around Charlotte for being an adroit businessman. In addition to the Clock & Watch, James Barren was also a leading civic leader. He was an Elder for his church, and was on several committees in Mecklenburg County.

In 1938, James Barren and his wife, Marge, welcomed their only child, Walter, into the world. Walter was raised in the Clock & Watch, charming customers with his adolescent ebullience. He would spend hours joking and laughing with patrons. Sometimes, Walter would hide from his father among the items in the shop.

At first, James thought Walter was just a precocious child, adventuresome and intelligent. One night, though, after a weird episode with Walter, he began to wonder about his child. James thought perhaps Walter was going through a phase: the overactive imagination of a child whose life had been ruled by the chiming of the hour.

When Walter was fifteen, he began to take the shop more seriously, entering into an apprenticeship with his father. He already knew quite a bit about the mechanics of timekeeping instruments, but he was not turning out to be the businessman his father had wanted. Walter worked with Edgar, one of the shop's salesmen, to learn how to close the deal on an important sale. Edgar had been hired by the elder Barren some years prior and was a reliable employee. Walter tried to pay as much attention to the balance sheets as to the balance scales, but he seemed destined to be only a mediocre salesman.

One day, in May of 1955, a new customer walked into the shop. Walter greeted him with a smile, but the customer, Mark A. Bellser, just stared at him with an annoyed look on his face. Walter knew this was going to be an unpleasant encounter. Mark Bellser, a short, round, bald man with an enormous ego, demanded not to see a clock, but to see Mr. Barren. Walter introduced Mr. Bellser to his father and quickly left the two men alone, not wanting to spend any more time than he had to in Mr. Bellser's company. In the months that followed, Mr. Bellser came into the shop several times. He was, without exception, rude and dismissive to Walter and Edgar, but pored sacrosanct praise on Mr. Barren. James did not much care for Mark A. Bellser, but Mr. Bellser did purchase several high-dollar timepieces. Although he was a wealthy and valued customer, James Barren always thought that Mr. Bellser was a slimy sycophant. James told Walter on more than one occasion that he thought Mr. Bellser just wanted to rub elbows with him for his business connections. The strained business relationship between James Barren, Walter, and Mark A. Bellser continued for several years. When James Barren passed away in 1959, Mr. Bellser did send a note of condolence, but Walter thought it more for show than genuine regret.

The elder Barren left the Clock & Watch to Walter, who ran it as best he could, before finally admitting that he needed to hire a manager to help

14: Clock & Watch

keep the books and pay the taxes. Walter Barren decided he would serve the shop best by sticking to the selection, care, and repair of the inventory. He interviewed several people, before eventually deciding on Rall Stringer. Walter liked Rall from the start and the two men worked well together. Several weeks after Mr. Barren's funeral, Mark Bellser came into the shop and looked around. With an arrogant smirk on his face, he turned to Walter and made a long and pointless statement about how much the shop had declined since the death of "his good friend, Mr. Barren." Mr. Bellser continued by belittling Walter and Rall, calling them incompetent laborers and stating that he hoped the shop would die alongside Mr. Barren.

Walter and Rall were both stunned at Mark Bellser's unwarranted attack on their business prowess. They concluded that Mr. Bellser had purchased the items to make inroads into the Charlotte business community through James Barren, not as a collector of fine antique pieces. They surmised that when the elder Barren passed, Mr. Bellser felt his social and business ambitions threatened. The two men rationalized the berating, but were still insulted and mad at Mr. Bellser's meanness.

That was not the end of it either. Over the next several months, Walter got word that Mark A. Bellser was gossiping about the shop and its employees all over town. While some people dismissed the harsh words from Mr. Bellser as out of proportion, business did seem to decline. Charlotte was growing and a couple of other clock shops had opened.

Walter and Rall, along with Edgar, loved what they were doing, but they also needed to get things back on track. Walter and Rall began having long conversations about the future of the shop. They agreed on most things, but not on every point. As time went on, they quarreled about petty differences in management practices. They tried to contain themselves in front of patrons, but they did receive some complaints from customers, who were annoyed at the indiscrete disagreements.

Edgar, for the most part, stayed out of these arguments, continuing to work quietly and steadily for the company. He only occasionally stepped in with a suggestion or point of view. The strain between Walter and Rall widened when a creditor came to the shop one afternoon for an in-person review. The creditor was a tall, thin man with pale skin and a strange birthmark on his cheek. Aside from his being a creditor, Walter disliked the man. After the man left the shop, Edgar listened to Walter and Rall argue in the back office for over an hour.

Over the next several days, Walter and Rall hardly spoke. Finally, they agreed to meet at Walter's home to work out a plan for the Clock & Watch. They both loved the shop and wanted to see it succeed. Joan Barren, Walter's new wife, cooked dinner and the three of them sat down for a pleasant

The Clock & Watch.

evening. They discussed mostly the shop, but other things as well. When dinner was over, the two men retired to the den to discuss their plans. Walter stretched his arms over his head and yawned. He glanced at the clocks in the den; it was long after midnight. Walter and Rall staged a plan, and Rall left Walter's house to return home. They finalized the details secretively over the next six days. The two men had agreed to implement the plan the next weekend.

    The plan called for them to break into Mark A. Bellser's house. The two of them would break in and steal the clocks that Bellser had purchased from the shop. Not only could they resell the clocks for an enormous profit, but the theft would also be revenge for Bellser's prior treatment of them. They might even steal other antiques from Bellser and sell them on the underground market. After all, he deserved what he got for treating them with such disrespect.

    They arrived at Mr. Bellser's house around 10:30 the next Friday night. They parked around the corner from the front gate, to avoid suspicion. The neighborhood was dark and quiet as Walter and Rall slipped in through the back fence. Carefully, they surveyed the house, studying where it would be easiest to enter. At long length, they decided on the kitchen window. Neither man had been in the house before, nor did they know their way

14: Clock & Watch

around. As luck would have it, a pocketknife was all Walter needed to get the window latch unlocked. Once inside, they crouched behind a large chest to see if the Bellsers, or anyone else in the house, had been aroused. After the house had remained quiet for several minutes, the two men moved into the living room. The Bellser house was a large colonial home with lots of dark corners and imposing passageways. Walter suggested they split and look separately; he would go upstairs, while Rall would look around downstairs and in the cellar.

As Rall was moving away, Walter grabbed him by the shirtsleeve. "Be sure to find the receipts…we need to destroy those receipts, so Bellser can't prove he owned the clocks," whispered Walter into Rall's ear.

"I know, I know," replied Rall. "Tell you what, I'll go through the desk and find the receipts, you gather the clocks," said Rall. Walter agreed.

Rall started searching the living room. He first looked through the oak chest that sat near the front door, but he found nothing of interest. He then slithered into the kitchen; people often hid things in cookie jars and junk drawers. Rall took care to be as quiet as he could, his search lit only by the glowing moonlight. Meanwhile, Walter had moved quietly upstairs. At the head of the stairs, he saw one of the clocks that he was looking for. He slowly took it down off the wall and placed it on a blanket he had left at the stairs. As he stood up, he recognized a table clock and added it to the first one on the blanket. Further down the hall, he saw the expensive silver scale his father had sold Bellser some years prior. A faintly radiating lamp was all the light Walter had to work with in the hallway. As Walter moved toward the silver scale, he became frozen into rigidity by the sound of a metal object clanging on the hardwood floor downstairs. On the first floor, Rall had accidentally knocked a fork onto the kitchen floor. Walter, upon hearing the sound, squeezed himself into a blackened corner to hide in the shadows of the hallway light. Deathly silence spread like sunset throughout the house. A single drop of sweat fell onto Walter's shirt. After several painful minutes, Walter proceeded with great caution toward the silver scale.

Downstairs, Rall picked up the fork, put it back where it had been, and walked into the hallway that led to Bellser's office. With the skill of a hunter, Rall slid into the office and admired the large ornate desk imposing its authority on the exactly proportioned room. Rall noted that there were several glass-fronted cabinets he would need to go through, as well as an antique coffee table. To avoid being heard upstairs, Rall carefully closed the office door. A large Oriental rug silenced Rall's footsteps as he crossed the room.

Suddenly, Walter was interrupted by the clicking of a door latch. Before he could fully engage his thoughts, Mark A. Bellser stood before him, gun in hand. It took a second or less for Mr. Bellser to recognize Walter in the dim light of the hallway.

Walter panicked and lunged at Mr. Bellser, knocking both men to the floor just inside Mr. Bellser's bedroom. The two men struggled for control of the gun. In the course of the struggle, Walter kicked the heavy bedroom door and it slowly glided shut. Mrs. Bellser watched from the four-poster bed in horror as her husband fought with the stranger, for she had not realized the intruder was Walter Barren.

Meanwhile, downstairs, Rall had found the receipt box and put its contents into his satchel. In the desk, he had also found several pocketwatches and a couple of pocketknives, and he put those in the bag.

While Rall ransacked Mr. Bellser's office, Walter was fighting for his life. Eventually, Walter was able to break free of Bellser's grip long enough to hit him in the mouth. Mr. Bellser fell limp to the floor with a broken jaw. A dreamlike trance took over Walter's mind. Upon seeing her husband go down, Mrs. Bellser let out a scream to wake the dead. Walter spun toward her and jumped with the fierceness of a lion. As he sprung across the bed, Walter felt himself come out of his own mind. He grabbed her by the throat and slung her to the floor on the far side of the bed. So hard had he squeezed and wretched her neck that it was broken in a matter of seconds. Walter stared down at the newly created corpse of Mrs. Bellser, mind racing. He had not entered the house with the intent of killing anyone, only to seek revenge for the condemnation of his reputation. In frustration of his own situation, Walter kicked Mrs. Bellser's corpse in the face to assure himself she was actually dead.

As the chimes of midnight rang throughout the house, Walter's thoughts then returned to Mr. Bellser, who was still lying unconscious on the floor. Walter thought of the gun, but he did not want anything so loud as to attract the attention of the neighbors. He looked around the room for some other type of weapon. Mr. Bellser's own cane would do just fine. As the last chime of the midnight hour reverberated in his mind, Walter rammed the cane through Mr. Bellser's left eye; lodging it deep into his brain. The weight of the cane jerked Bellser's head sharply to his left. Walter just grinned at the sound of the cane's metal handle smacking the floor. He stared in sinister glee at the blood that had spilled out onto the floorboards and was seeping through the cracks. In a morose gesture of morbid celebration, Walter yanked the cane out of Bellser's eye and slung it at the open armoire. It spewed blood across the room as it crashed into the neatly hung clothes without making hardly a sound.

Walter needed to reconcile that he was now a murderer, as well as a thief, and so he took a moment to gather his thoughts. To Walter, the whole

14: Clock & Watch

episode with the Bellsers in their bedroom had seemed more like some nightmare than reality. Once he felt composed, he continued gathering clocks and watches in the other bedrooms with abandon.

Meanwhile, Rall was still in the office and had not heard a thing upstairs. He finished his search of the office and decided to meet up with Walter upstairs. As he made his way up the stairwell, he noticed Walter in the doorway to the attic. The two men nodded at each other. Walter turned to ascend the attic stairs, but stopped short, turned to Rall, and said, "We have the house to ourselves." He then vanished into the attic.

Rall grinned, but wondered what Walter had meant by that statement. Rall turned toward a large door at the end of the hallway and proceeded toward it.

No sooner had he taken his first step than a nearly transparent figure appeared before him in the doorway. The figure was short and bald, wearing silk pajamas and a custom bathrobe. The ghastly figure had a badly displaced jaw and its left eye was missing. Shiny red blood slowly gushed from the empty eye socket, but disappeared as it fell. Rall's first thought was that they had started a fire and that he was looking at smoke wafting through the hall. Then, just as suddenly as the first ghostly figure had appeared, a second figure emerged from the master bedroom. This second figure was of an older woman with her head cocked to the right in an excruciatingly awkward manner, a hollow staring to her eyes. Her throat seemed twisted far out of its normal proportions. She seemed to glow an eerie tombstone grey.

Since Rall had not known that Walter had murdered the Bellsers, to see them now in ghostly form was almost more than Rall's heart could take. He felt faint. Both figures began to move toward Rall, who fell backward onto the floor. He opened his eyes to see the ghost of Mr. Bellser leaning over him with the bloody cane raised as if to strike him. He let out a scream and the looming figures vanished. When he again opened his eyes, the wafting image of the Bellsers was nearly upon him. As if he were listening through water, Rall heard the ghost of Mr. Bellser shrieking threats at him. Rall was, by this time, completely embroiled in terror. He ran, collapsing on the foyer floor downstairs. When he looked over his shoulder, there was the menacing figure of Mrs. Bellser, arms outstretched toward him, fingers curved as if to strangle him. Rall scrambled across the floor into the living room. Arched out backward on the area rug, Rall quickly stared up into the enormous fireplace before him. The head of Mr. Bellser, upside down, appeared to glow like dying embers in the chimney flue.

The inverted head said, "You will never escape my wrath!"

Rall passed out. He awoke a few minutes later to a deathly silent house. Quickly, he made his way back upstairs and found the attic door ajar. He reached out for the knob, but saw only the pallid gray hand of Mr. Bellser in its place. The digits curled slowly inward, as if to dare him to touch them. With all the courage he could muster, Rall ran past the creepy hand and up the stairs into the attic. There he found mostly darkness, with only a few slivers of light casting shadows on the dusty attic floor.

Soon, he found Walter leaned over a large chest. Rall frantically tapped Walter on the shoulder. Walter stood and looked at Rall, unable to read his face in the half-light of the attic. Rall blurted out his story of the ghosts in the hallway, ending his rant by asking Walter if he knew what had happened to the Bellsers.

Walter simply replied, "I murdered them."

Rall turned and ran, head dizzy with fright and confusion. Rall headed downstairs and into a small room off the kitchen. Not seconds after he had entered the room, the angry ghost of Mrs. Bellser blocked the doorway. Rall just stared at the specter in the doorway, and then, as if that were not enough, the barely illuminated figure of Mr. Bellser came through the doorway, through Mrs. Bellser, into the room. Mr. Bellser raised his cane over his bleeding head as if to strike. Rall passed out for a second time.

He awoke sometime later, Walter shaking him by the shoulder. "I brought you out onto the patio so you could get some fresh air," Walter said to Rall upon his regaining consciousness. "You were passed out in a small room; you had been ranting loquaciously about spirits of the dead tormenting you," said Walter. "I, for one, saw no ghosts…and, since I was the one to kill them, would they not have come after me?"

Rall just glared at Walter. "All this…for a clock shop? You would murder someone over an insult?" I came to steal clocks and receipts, not to be company to murder! How dare you drag me into this! I'm ringing the police!" He stormed off, back into the house and down the hallway.

In the chiming of the two o'clock hour, Rall was dead.

Quickly, Walter gathered up the clocks and scales, the satchel of receipts, and the other items. He packed the booty carefully into his car, checked the Bellser house one last time, and returned to his own home. Walter was finishing unpacking the clocks at his house when they began to chime three in the morning.

Walter, at first, breathed in deeply, enjoying the precious sound of those beautiful chimes. He dreamed of how he could make thousands on them. He also smirked in self-satisfaction at his revenge against the Bellsers. Rall… well, Rall was an unfortunate case.

The continued chiming of the clocks broke Walters dream-like state. He looked at his own wristwatch; it was ten after three in the morning. The clocks should be silent. Why were they still chiming? Chiming, chiming

14: Clock & Watch

The front door of The Clock & Watch.

like the "Bells" of Edgar Allen Poe! Chiming, chiming like the insistent pawing of a cat at a closed door. Walter checked each clock, each one's mechanics as still as a corpse in its coffin. However, still, he heard the chiming, the endless chiming. As the moon crept across the night, Walter's mind became consumed by the chiming in his ears.

Meanwhile, Edgar was awoken in his own bed by a sound. He sat up and looked around his darkened room. He listened to the sound of his wife's breathing, while he gave his eyes a couple minutes to adjust to the miniscule amount of light.

Must have been that weather vane I need to oil, he thought to himself. Edgar settled his head back on his pillow, only to be startled by the sudden appearance of a specter floating over his bed. He let out a scream that made no sound. The phantasmal spirit of Rall reached out and took Edgar by the hand. The spirit spoke to Edgar in cryptic waves of language. Edgar listened like an enraptured schoolboy. The ghost of Rall proceeded to tell Edgar of the robbery plot, the murder of the Bellsers, and of his own demise at the hands of Walter. In stunning and articulate detail, he recounted the evening's events.

While still staring at the ghost of Rall, Edgar woke his wife and asked, "Honey, do you see anything strange?" The phantom disappeared in to the darkness of the room.

"No dear; what do you mean?" Edgar proceeded to tell his wife of the vision he had just had of Rall—and of the robbery and of the murders. He recounted to her in vivid detail the plot and scheme.

His wife replied, "Edgar, it must have been a dream; go back to sleep."

Edgar stared at the ceiling for the reminder of the night.

In the morning, Edgar got up early. He was tired, and more than a bit shaken by Rall's ghostly presence over his bed. He got dressed and left the house without breakfast. When he arrived at the Clock & Watch, he found the front door securely locked and undisturbed. Everything was normal in the shop. Edgar nervously waited for Walter to arrive. When, by eleven, he had not arrived, Edgar called the police. They searched the shop, but found nothing.

The police chief, Morton Dallhern, decided to go to Walter's house, just in case. Upon arriving at Walter's house, Chief Dallhern knocked on the door with no reply.

Just then, officer Mells said, "Chief, I see someone through the dining room window."

Chief Dallhern knocked for a second time. He then decided to break in the door to investigate. The police officers found Walter curled up in a corner of the dining room, clutching an antique mantle clock and madly

14: Clock & Watch

rambling about a one-eyed ghost and a vicious female figure that kept appearing and disappearing before his eyes. He told the police of the endless incessant chiming in his head. Walter told the police that the ghostly figures were trying to kill him. In his terror, Walter confessed to the robbery and murders at the Bellser house. He claimed, too, that he had killed Rall to stop him from reporting the crimes to the police. Walter rambled for quite a while about ghosts and other unworldly visions.

While two officers watched over Walter at his house, Chief Dallhern and several other officers went to the home of Mr. Bellser. There they found a clockless house and three dead bodies: in the upstairs master bedroom, the bodies of Mr. and Mrs. Bellser, just as Walter had described them; on the back patio, the body of Rall Stringer, right where Walter said it would be.

Walter was arrested, charged with three counts of murder and one count of robbery. Being that the murders took place in the course of a robbery, the case was designated a capital offense. The prosecution sought the death penalty.

Walter sat in his jail cell screaming to the walls about a couple of ghosts that were in his cell. Day after day, he mumbled in a psychopathic rant about murderous spirits that were after him. He was finally taken away to the state asylum for evaluation. His lucid moments earned him a "sane" designation and he went to trial. The prosecution's case was simple. Walter Barren had murdered the Bellsers while robbing their home. He was found in possession of their clocks in his own house. The prosecutor even had the receipts with Bellser's name, address, and signature to prove it all. Walter's defense lawyer nodded his head in uncharacteristic agreement. He offered almost no defense. Though Walter claimed to be innocent of the murders, a conviction was swift, and final.

Three months later, Walter Barren was executed by the state of North Carolina. Given a chance to speak, he said only the fear of being let loose in the spirit world with the Bellsers scared him. After the execution and pronouncement of death, he was buried in the family gravesite near Fern Creek. The nearly constant storm cloud over his grave in the days after his burial led some to surmise that the Bellsers were still haunting Walter.

Closed during the trial, Edgar opened the Clock & Watch some days after Walter was laid to rest. He figured the publicity from the trial would lead to a renewed interest in the shop. He was right. For days, the shop was full of new customers. Edgar soon realized that most of them were there to gossip about the trial and execution of Walter Barren—not to buy clocks.

At the end of his fourteenth day back at work, Edgar locked the front door, and made his way to the back of the shop and entered the stockroom, only to be confronted by a very angry ghost. The ghost of Walter Barren floated before him. Walter's ghost appeared more like flames in a fireplace than curls of soft white smoke. Walter's burning hand reached out and grabbed Edgar by the throat, pinning him with fear against a set of shelves. Edgar tried to speak, but Walter's death growl voice overwhelmed him. Edgar could smell the retched scent of burning hair. The ends of his beard were burning where Walter's enraged hand was clasping his throat.

Walter's ghost said to Edgar, "In the spirit world, all is revealed—things on earth seem one way, but are often another." Walter continued, "I see across the universe to all right and wrong, and although I claim fault in wanting to rob from the Bellsers, I went there with only the intent to rob them, and that is all I did. I broke into the house, I stole the scales and clocks, and I punched Mr. Bellser in the jaw. The all-seeing Lord knows I did those things, but the Lord knows, and I now know, that it was you, Edgar…that stole the souls of Mr. and Mrs. Bellser from your world and sent them to the world in which I now find myself. You, Edgar, overheard Rall and I plotting the robbery and you decided it was an opportunity for you to take over the Clock & Watch. You slipped into the Bellser's house after us. You murdered the Bellsers in their bedroom while Rall and I were somewhere else in the house. You, Edgar, murdered Rall to get him out of the way of the shop, so you could take it over! How dare you let the state execute me for a murder I did not commit! I am a robber, Edgar, but you are a murderer, and I shall terrorize you until you until you join me on this side of the eternal curtain!"

"In local news…" The pretty blonde reporter said into the camera, "a downtown business burned to the ground last night in a massive fire, under what police are calling 'mysterious circumstances.'" The reporter continued, with an oddly cynical smile on her face. "Barren's Clock & Watch, known in the neighborhood simply as 'Clock & Watch,' was a longstanding business that sold clocks, scales, and watches to customers in Charlotte for over thirty years. It was most recently in the news as part of a bizarre murder trial involving its then owner, Walter Barren. Barren was, viewers may remember, recently executed for three murders. The shop caught fire sometime last night right after closing. Police have recovered one, as yet unidentified, body. Police think the body belongs to a shop employee named Edgar, but are waiting on confirmation from the coroner. Now to William for the weather…"

15
Ginger's Bridge

Ginger Peterson was depressed. She had been dating Larry for over two years when he suddenly broke up with her. He gave no real explanation for the break up, no warning that anything was wrong. His motives were as unclear as the murky water seventy feet beneath her. Ginger thought that the relationship was headed in the right direction. As she looked out over the Catawba River from the bridge, her mind canvassed every memory to try to figure out where it all went wrong. Ginger liked to come to the bridge; it was her place to think, and today she needed to think.

They had talked about getting married and having children. She and Larry had trusted each other with their dreams and fears, their difficulties and triumphs. Why now, she thought? Was it some other woman? Was it expectation? She had always thought that they saw eye-to-eye on most things. As Ginger thought more and more about it, her mind moved from explanation to explanation. Her emotions vacillated wildly between confusion and anger.

Meanwhile, Larry was sitting at home wondering about the afternoon's events. Had he done the right thing? He had not meant to hurt her feelings; he just wanted to date other women—and cheating was not the right way to go about it. It was not that he disliked Ginger; it was just that he was young and wanted to explore other options. In many ways, Larry loved Ginger, and hoped that they could be, at least, close friends.

Larry, at last, fell into a restless sleep on his couch. Bad dreams plagued his unconsciousness. From the moment he fell into the world between places, Larry was tormented by visions of Ginger. Not the normal Ginger, but a

Ginger he hardly recognized. A Ginger with her face contorted beyond her own. He could see the veins in her hands turn black as they crept around her fingers. She spun in swirls of wrath. In his dream, Larry fell to the ground, as if some enormous weight was holding him between gravity and suspension. The tips of his toes began to turn a sick, greyish-green. He felt himself being pulled into some nefarious wetness. As the strange water engulfed him, unearthly things brushed against his arms and legs. Larry gasped for air, but the place he now found himself was a world of imminent liquid suffocation. Without warning, Larry felt himself being hit from behind by some large, hard object.

Larry woke up on the floor of his apartment. He had fallen off the couch in reaction to his dream. Just as he was shaking his head, Larry heard his phone ring. His best friend was calling to tell him to turn on the nightly news. A report was saying some girl who looked like Ginger had jumped off the bridge. The bridge, which spanned the Catawba River, was notorious for suicides. He tried calling Ginger, but no one answered. As Larry ran out the door towards his car, he hoped beyond hope that the girl in the report was not Ginger. He hoped, in fact, that the report was false altogether. Larry hopped into his car, grabbed the steering wheel, and began to drive like a maniac towards the bridge. Due to police cars blocking the street, two blocks was as close as Larry could get. He ran the remainder of the distance to the bridge. It was marked off by yellow police tape and an on duty officer waved him away. Larry nearly vomited at the scene. Blue and white lights reflected like a flag of death off the bridge's support trusses. He begged the officer to let him through, but was unsuccessful. Eventually, Larry found his way onto the suspended sidewalk. At last, a police officer pointed to the bank below and said to Larry, "The victim is being taken out of the water now, down there."

He reached the scene just as the ambulance was pulling away to take someone to the hospital in Charlotte. He knew asking at the hospital would be pointless.

Larry begged a police officer to tell him what had happened, but the only information he could obtain said the victim was yet unidentified. Ginger's phone remained unanswered. He returned to his apartment to wait. The waiting drew out into hours. Larry again fell into the nightmare of his sleep. He found himself again floating in the waters of apprehension. Strange visions of Ginger's head attached to some horrid sea beast nearly drove him mad. The constant gushing of the puke-green waters drowned his last chance for a peaceful night. Finally, at around six in the morning, Larry's phone woke him from his fitful slumber.

15: Ginger's Bridge

The voice on the other end of the phone said, "Larry Plains, we need to talk."

Larry replied, "Who is this?"

The voice said, "This is Police Chief Kawaka, of the Charlotte Police Department."

"What do you want?" replied Larry.

"Do you know a girl named Cindy Molson?"

"No," said Larry.

"Well, she apparently knew you. She left a suicide note addressed to you last night before jumping off the bridge," replied Chief Kawaka. "You'd better come down to the station."

"Yes sir," said Larry.

Upon arriving at the station forty-five minutes later, Larry was escorted to an interview room. There he told the police about Ginger, the break up, the episode on the bridge, the nightmares, and his being asked about Cindy Molson. The police asked Larry why he thought a girl who did not even know him was referencing him in a suicide note. The police openly wondered if Larry was telling them the whole truth. Had he been dating Cindy secretively, while also dating Ginger? Where was Ginger?

Larry thought, *Where is Ginger?* That was a damn fine question. He asked the police to find her; if they could find Ginger, they might find the underlying cause of this. Larry headed back to his apartment, wondering all the while about the missing Ginger. He tried calling her phone several more times during the day and waited on the police to call him if they found anything. By mid-afternoon, he decided to pay Ginger a visit.

He knocked on her door, but no one answered. Larry could not see much of anything through the windows. As he leaned over a shrub to try and get a better look in the living room, his phone rang, nearly causing him to fall over. It was Ginger.

"Where are you?" Larry asked. "The police and I are looking for you."

Ginger coldly replied, "I went to spend the night at my mom's house in Columbus; I was upset at our break up."

"Oh," replied Larry. He then proceeded to tell Ginger about the cops, the note, and Cindy, the girl who committed suicide on the bridge.

Ginger had an oddly unsympathetic reply, "Well, maybe you deserve it."

Larry did not know quite what she meant by that, but he let it slide. "I'll talk with you later," he said to Ginger. Hanging up the phone, he called Police Chief Kawaka, to tell him he had spoken with Ginger.

Chief Kawaka said, "We still need to know about you and Cindy Molson."

"I swear I don't know a Cindy Molson, Chief," Larry replied.

The view from Ginger's Bridge gives no clue about the horrific events of that night.

"Okay," said Police Chief Kawaka suspiciously.

Larry hung up the phone and hoped that was the end of it.

The next several days passed slowly for Larry; the events of that night bothered him tremendously. He had hoped to be free to do some dating, but dating was the last thing on his mind now.

The next Thursday, Larry decided to go back to the bridge. He wanted to get some closure, or at least some sense of understanding. The clouds were thick and dark in the sky over the bridge when Larry arrived. He looked up at the impending storm and thought to himself, *How appropriate.*

Just then, a familiar face appeared on the bridge.

"Hey man, what are you doing out here?" Don, Larry's best friend, said.

"Oh, it's you," Larry replied. The two men stood on the bridge and talked for over an hour, but the conversation did not make Larry feel much better.

Eventually, Don said, "Well, I've gotta go; I'll talk with you later." With that, Don left.

No sooner had Don walked away than Larry turned to see a girl on the bridge. He did not recognize her, and only gave her the slightest smile of acknowledgment. Larry looked away, not wanting to be thought of as staring. He looked back a moment later, only to see the girl standing near him, glaring at him with an angry stare. A crash of thunder split the sky at that

15: Ginger's Bridge

moment, striking terror into Larry's heart. The girl looked vaguely like Ginger, but closer to the girl Police Chief Kawaka described as Cindy Molson.

Almost as soon as she had appeared, the girl was gone. Larry heard a loud splash in the river below him. His mind was taken over by fear and surprise. Had that girl jumped in and committed suicide right before him? Dare he look over the rail? Was he imagining things?

At that inopportune moment, another girl appeared on the bridge, this time on the opposing side. She, too, looked similar to Ginger—or Cindy.

She pointed to Larry and screamed, "Get off my bridge!"

Like the first girl, she also jumped up on the rail. She crouched and waved goodbye to Larry. Without thinking, Larry darted out into traffic, in an effort to reach the girl before she went over. Larry was jarred by the sound of screeching tires. He waved to the car to pass as he looked up at the empty rail. As he looked over the side, he saw the hands of the young girl quickly submerge below the surface of the murky, green water.

Larry started to jump in after her, but was distracted by yet another girl along the rail. "Help me!" she cried out, extending her arm to Larry. He ran toward her, only to see her disappear over the edge of the rail and into the waiting water. Just about out of his mind, Larry spun around, only to see Ginger standing on the opposing sidewalk.

All other thoughts cleared his mind, as he singly focused on Ginger. Maybe she could explain all this. He ran toward her, barely escaping death by car. As he arrived on the sidewalk near Ginger, he noticed that she was not quite herself.

"Ginger?" Larry asked aloud in panicked waves of sound. He ran toward her, arms outstretched. When he got to her, he reached out to hug her, only to fall hard against one of the trusses. When Larry regained consciousness, he saw that a group of girls who resembled Ginger surrounded him. Each one of them was calling out to him, just before jumping off the bridge into the water below. Frozen in terror, Larry watched as Ginger after Ginger jumped into the murky, churning water.

He passed out from fright, only to wake to a single girl standing over him. The light was becoming scarce as the sun set to the west, but in the dusk, Larry could barely make out the face of the girl standing before him. Was it Ginger who stood before him, or was it Cindy? He could not tell the girls apart. Their faces seemed to morph together, as if they were one in the same.

Larry lost all sense of reality. He staggered to his feet and grabbed the rail. Before he knew it, he was falling into the water below. The death-grey water swallowed him completely, as a mausoleum enshrines a casket. What senses he had left were quickly consumed by the waters that pulled him first to the right and then to the left. Horrible things brushed up against him as he floated in the waters of supernatural dementia. He was submerged in the currents of his previous dream; his watery nightmare had come true. The muddy bottom of the Catawba River grabbed at Larry's feet. Struggling to see in the dark waters, a face suddenly came clearly into view. The bloated, eaten face of Ginger appeared in the swirling waters. Suddenly, bony skinless fingers reached out and grabbed Larry. He struggled to resist, but the ghostly corpse of Ginger held on tightly.

Local legend says that Larry and Ginger are still, to this day, under Ginger's bridge, struggling with each other beneath the surface of the river.

16
Winter

Cold is the winter wind.

Here I am, with trowel in hand, contemplating burying that which winter plans to kill.

I sway uneasily upon my feet, here with the day of fools upon me, clenching a fist that had meant to break the frozen soil's stranglehold.

The grave before which I stand is heaved as heavy as mine lungs from the vacillation of the season's whims.

As crystals form along my muscle tissue, my nearly, but not quite, paralyzed mind at long length realizes that I am as bereft of intent as the coming of the spring.

My impetuous walk in vain.

The languidly dying ghosts of winter still ensnare my neck and sleeve, pulling me into a desperate chill that only my heart has known til now…

For how can the warming winds of her beauty blossom when the death knell of winter's wrath has yet to ring.

Save me…save me! I cried out with raspy voice into the icy breath of Mother Nature's indifference! Save me…Save me!

However, my pleas, alas, fell on senses as deaf as the still dead earth's unopened flowers.

Oh, how I am haunted by the winter's wind.

~Roy Heizer

16: Winter

Winter.

17
The Factory

The old road that ran beside the factory was overrun with weeds and decaying leaves. No one in the neighborhood could remember the last time a delivery truck brought in supplies, much less the last day the workers were employed. The enormous metal structure had once been a thriving factory, producing steel products for a larger out-of-town metal conglomerate. The factory had once employed well over a thousand laborers. The jobs at the factory kept that small town on the outskirts of Charlotte going.

When the factory closed and the jobs went overseas in early 1970, the town was devastated. Because of the closing, shops and restaurants that depended on the factory were also forced to close. Many people left to find work in other towns. The once-proud sign out front was now cracked and rusting away; the building itself was not in any better condition. A chain on the gate had long since broken and left to dangle like a neglected rusty fob. One could stand outside the factory and smell rotting tobacco, mold, and sadness. It seemed the entire property was slowly falling into disrepair.

By the late 1990s, some prominent local citizens had decided to clean up various properties that were neglected. The town council members were upset that these properties were in tax default, dangerous to trespassers, and an eyesore of the community. They ordered them taken over by the county and torn down. The mayor proclaimed that the scrap metal and recovered materials could be sold off to pay for the demolition. Insurance regulations required an inspection of any property slated for demolition. A date was set for an inspection of the old metal factory, along with several other properties marked for removal.

17: The Factory

The factory in better times.

    The morning of the inspection rolled around, and several past and present council members arrived at the factory to find the inspector waiting for them outside the factory gates. Before they got started, the group drank coffee and discussed the inspection process. The chief insurance inspector, a tall, thin man named Cyrus Lavergne, shared with the group that he was a political buff and the property they were about to enter was said by some to have been built near the childhood home of former President James K. Polk. The factory and its extensive grounds were, in fact, rumored to be haunted by his ghost. Several of the council members laughed about the "noises and strange lights" that had been reported at the factory over the years. One council member even joked about how badly the Jaycees wanted to use it for their haunted house at Halloween. The property was, of course, far too dangerous for the public.
    The group of five men and three women started the inspection around ten in the morning. As they moved through the building, they were careful to watch for rotting floorboards and protruding objects that might be sharp. Not far into the inspection process, one of the women commented that she had never realized how dark it was inside the factory, even in the daytime. Everyone on the inspection crew wore hardhats and carried flashlights. Since the building was to be demolished, the inspector was not so much looking at the structure, but other things. First, they needed to be sure no person was living in the factory, and, secondly, that no dangerous chemicals were present. The group had agreed to split up and meet back at the front door in three hours for lunch. A group of locals, one man and the three

The lot where the factory once stood.

women, headed off down one of the corridors to see if they could find any evidence that someone was living in the abandoned structure. The other four men, including Cyrus Lavergne, started their inspection in the opposite direction; they were looking for chemicals.

The first group made their way across a large open area that was filthy, only to be met on the far side by an imposing set of double doors. The dusty sign over the door read: "Break room–Restrooms–Showers."

Don Krater looked at the three women and said, "The water has not been on in here for years, I'm sure the showers and restrooms are useless. I don't, however, know if squatters have ravaged the place."

The women agreed.

When the group got to the restroom doors, Don said, "I'll go in here; you ladies inspect the women's room."

The women nodded their heads in unison and they went their separate ways. Small slivers of light came into the women's restroom through the cracks in the boarded-up windows. The three women held each other's arms, only slightly more curious than afraid. Only half of the eight individual stalls had doors on them, while three of the toilets were already demolished. The women agreed that there was no sign of a vagrant in the women's restroom and so they decided to call that room finished.

They walked back to the hallway to wait for Don. They waited and

17: The Factory

waited and waited, but Don did not emerge from the men's room. Finally, they decided to go in and look for him. The men's room was vacant. The entire break area was also vacant, except for an old pile of clothes in the corner that looked like it had been there for years. The women thought perhaps Don had gone exploring elsewhere in the building. They went to look for him.

Meanwhile, the other group was busy cataloging some barrels they had found on a different floor. Mr. Lavergne would take a sample out and smell it, to see if it was familiar. The other men took notes and bantered about how the Buckeyes were doing that season. Eventually, they moved on through the darkness of the space. Several times, members of the team cried out in disgust as they broke through a cobweb, or brushed up against something they could not see. The inspection team moved to the floor just below the barrels, only to find the chemicals had formed stalactites of grossness through the factory floor. The factory was enormous and the teams did not run into each other during their respective searches. They only had radio contact with the other team and it was not long before the news of Don's disappearance came through to the lead team. The inspection had now taken on a much more mysterious dynamic. Soon after the radio announcement, Mr. Lavergne's team made its way into a creepy room that looked like it contained a set of small closets.

"Weird," said one of the team members to Mr. Lavergne.

"I agree," replied Cyrus. "My father would…" Mr. Lavergne stopped in the middle of his sentence and pointed up at something on the wall. The other members of the team turned to look in the direction that Mr. Lavergne was pointing.

"I don't see anything," said Doug, Mr. Lavergne's assistant.

"Neither do I," echoed the remaining men on the team.

"Must be a shadow; let us move on," said Mr. Lavergne.

The group walked on through the darkness, following the irregular glow of their flashlights.

As the lead team looped around and approached the set of double doors marked "Break room–Restrooms–Showers," Doug remarked that this must be where the women had been when they radioed about Don.

"Yes, we need to double check in there," said Mr. Lavergne.

At that moment, the radio crackled with a woman's voice, "We have not found Don… also…we think we may be lost, we can't find the door we came in through," the voice said.

"Okay," said Mr. Lavergne, "We'll look for you when we are through in the Break room area."

The radio fell silent.

The team headed by Cyrus Lavergne began to inspect the two restrooms and the break area. The men made several notes about the condition of the restrooms, but found nothing out of the ordinary in either one. They, too, found nothing in the break area except the pile of old clothes. The four men stood for a long time and stared at the pile.

Eventually, Cyrus said, "Doug, pick up those clothes, we need to see what's under them."

Doug looked at Cyrus with a questioning stare, but he reached down, snagged the first item on top, and disappeared into the pile. Without thinking, one of the other men on the team reached out for Doug, only to disappear into the pile of clothes himself.

The only remaining man in the group turned to Mr. Lavergne and screamed, "Did you see that?"

Lavergne immediately grabbed the man by the shirtsleeve and slung him forcibly onto the pile of clothes. Upon hitting the pile, the man vanished like the others as Cyrus Lavergne cracked a gleeful sinister grin.

Somewhere else in the factory, the three women searched for signs of life. They crept down a long dark workroom with flashlights shining in every direction. Shards of rusty metal pointed out at them like metallic fingers on an industrial skeleton. Curious about the building, and about Don, the women pressed on. After more than an hour of searching, one of the women sat down on a bench that was thick with dust. She needed to catch her breath, but ended up weeping into her hands as the two other women comforted her. It seemed the fact Don had just disappeared into the walls of the dank old factory was more than she could handle. With pursed lips and a hard exhale, the woman stood up, straightened her blouse, and said firmly, "Okay, we need to move on." The two other women agreed.

"Don!?" The women cried out as they walked from area to area. By the time the three women reached the fifth floor, they were exhausted, but glad to see some slivers of light coming through a small row of windows on what looked to be the north side of the factory. In the day's only moment of levity, one of the women pointed out that she could see the road from the window and remarked how nice it was to see sunlight.

"What time is it?" one of the women asked.

"Almost one; we'll need to meet Lavergne at the front door, near the gate soon," said another of the women in reply. "Let's head downstairs then, it may take us a while to find our way out of here."

The group headed towards the stairs. "Besides, Don knows to meet us at the gates for lunch; I'm sure we'll all laugh about this then."

When the three women arrived at the gate twenty minutes late, no one was there. No Don, no Cyrus, not anyone. They had been there for a couple

17: The Factory

minutes when one of the women noticed a strange greenish-blue light emanating from a missing section of the sheet metal wall near where they stood. The women looked around to see if anyone was coming. When they were sure they were alone, they pressed their faces up to the open section of the wall. The light seemed to be at the far end of a long corridor; they stepped back inside the factory to get a better look.

Suddenly, as if they had been drawn into some sort of space ripple, the three women found themselves in a dark place they did not recognize. Out of nowhere, Cyrus Lavergne appeared. The eerie light glowed all around him like some badly backlit shadow.

Later that evening, when none of the council members had returned home, their families began to make phone calls around town. An official police search to try to find the missing people was launched before midnight. A long, nervous night of waiting unfolded before the families. The town was in a near panic by morning, when none of the officers assigned to the case had turned up or reported to their station. Radio contact was not established and the morning sun was met by a throng of people at the gate. All of them demanded answers. Eventually, an officer from the next town over asked the question, "Who is this insurance inspector Cyrus Lavergne, anyway?" No one knew the answer.

A couple of police officers were sent to his office downtown. They knocked on the door, but no one answered. One of the officers said, "I think he has a window at the back, we could look in."

The two officers went around to the back of the building. There, to their surprise, they found a body lying dead in the parking lot beside his car. His keys were still clenched tightly in his cold, grey hand. An autopsy done later that day identified the corpse as that of Cyrus Lavergne. The autopsy report came back marked as INCONCLUSIVE. The only thing the coroner could say for sure was that Mr. Lavergne had been dead for almost three days.

The bodies of the missing council members were never found. The officers investigating their missing persons' case were never found. No official answer was ever given for the disappearances. The factory was gated up and, some months later, torn down by means of remote explosion.

The rumors and stories swirled like a hurricane of gossip around the case. Was it a crime? Was it corporate mischief? Was it an alien from outer space? Was the factory a portal to another world? Was it some sort of ghost out for revenge? To this day, those questions remain unanswered.

18
Fred Mirkoff

Fred Mirkoff had always loved staring up at the stars. Ever since he had been a small child growing up in the suburbs of Charlotte he had wanted to interact with the planets and constellations in the night sky. He would spend hours, when he should have been sleeping, staring out into the world of glittering lights beyond his own. Fred disliked cloudy nights; those nights, his mother would explain, were the nights when his friends in the distance were not allowed to come out and play. On those nights, he would hide under his sheets with a flashlight and read comic books about spaceships or flying saucers from across time and space.

Fred's life in Charlotte was difficult; school was hard for him. The other kids picked on him, he had no close friends, and to top it all off, things at home were strained. Fred's father worked as a mountain ranger, and he was gone for long stretches at a time. His overworked mother tried to make the best of things, but a tight household budget and stress made her grouchy with Fred and his three older sisters occasionally. World War II caused its own set of economic problems in the Mirkoff household during Fred's middle school years, as all Charlotte families had to ration things.

To escape his home life, Fred would stay up late into the night, listening to the voice on the radio spin tales of aliens from outer space. In the daytime, when his celestial friends were asleep, Fred would read the latest stories of scientific progress in astronomy and science magazines. He knew his parents had no money to buy astronomy equipment, and so young Fred would spend many lonely hours walking around the neighborhood, gathering anything he thought he could use to make a telescope. He kept a large journal of all

18: Fred Mirkoff

In another world...

his scientific exploits, newspaper clippings of the days' astrology readings, and a list of experiments he carried out in the garage. Fred even managed to beg an occasional book on astronomy or astrology off the high school librarian. If the weather did not permit observations or the garage was too cold to preform experiments, Fred would spend his time studying the folklore behind the constellations. In 1949, real life in Charlotte was filled with poverty and the hardships of Appalachian life; Fred's life, however, was a wonderful mixture of science and astrological mythology.

Mr. Mirkoff, a first generation Russian immigrant, wanted his son to concentrate on more earthly matters. He knew about the pressures that a Russian-American would have to face given the reputation of Communism in America. He hoped his son would go to college and study Forestry or Dendrology, trades that might be useful in a state that was over eighty percent forest. Mr. Mirkoff stated more than once that he would be happy if young Fred studied mine engineering, so he might at least put that scientific mind of his to good use.

Fred had always wanted to go to college—not to study mine engineering, but to study astronomy. Whenever Fred and his father quarreled about his future, Fred would just focus on his celestial friends that much more. In many ways, Fred trusted the stability and consistency of the heavenly world more than his earthly one. Despite their quarrels over career choices, Fred never questioned his father's love for his family.

Haunted Charlotte

One day, in 1950, when Fred was seventeen, his father was killed in a forestry accident involving a rockslide on one of Watauga County's steepest mountains. The death of Mr. Mirkoff left Fred's mother deeply depressed and in even greater financial strain. Fred's dream of college died with his father and he joined the maintenance crew at a local factory to make ends meet. The job at the factory was not all bad; it afforded Fred the chance to use his mechanical side and keep in tune with all sorts of machinery.

Jim Connolly, Fred's boss at the factory, liked his work, but complaints of daydreaming started almost immediately. Fred confessed that most of the time he was working on equipment, he was actually imagining himself working on a time travel machine that was on some spaceship in a galaxy far beyond this one. Despite the daydreaming, Jim thought Fred did excellent work and the two men came to the agreement that as long as the daydreaming helped Fred get through the day, it was fine with Jim. The factory was large and several dozen people were employed there, most of them locals who had known Fred all his life. Several of the older men had even, at one time or another, dated one of Fred's three older sisters. Fred settled into his routine and a couple years passed quickly.

One evening, Fred had the night off, and, still preoccupied with the stars, decided to sit on his porch and view his old friends through his new telescope. On that night, he saw a small blue light in the sky he had never noticed before. He adjusted the scope to narrow in on the strange blue light. As he honed in on the light, it began to change from blue to purple, and back to blue. It morphed in shape, changing from a spherical ball into a non-distinct shape before becoming more fluid in its formation. Fred pulled the lens as close to the object as he could, only to see the morphing glow continue to dance before him. He looked up with his naked eye in the direction of the shape, but he could see nothing without the aid of the telescope. This told Fred that the object—whatever it was—was very far away.

A few days later, when he looked again, he saw that the object had not left its position in the heavens, but continued to cast its eerie blue and purple glow. It did, though, seem somewhat larger than it had before, but Fred did not have the equipment for an exact measurement.

Over the next several days, Fred looked up the object in every book and magazine he owned, but found no reference to the morphing light source. None of his fellow astronomers had ever seen or heard about it. He had no idea what it was: a star, a planet, or maybe a spaceship with aliens on board? His imagination went wild over the prospect that he might have discovered a new celestial body or revealed an alien being.

18: Fred Mirkoff

Fred wrote a long letter about the object to the University of North Carolina's science department, but they too said they had no record of its existence. Fred began to wonder if it was all in his imagination. The light continued to appear in Fred's lens, growing slowly larger as the weeks passed. Within a month, nearly everything within Fred's telescopic view was bathed in the flowing blue light.

Then, just as clearly as the light itself had appeared, another object began to develop at the center of the light. A white-hot glow began to swell within the source of the illumination. Fred stared in enraptured wonder at the white light within the blue. As the white light continued to grow, Fred noticed a figure emerging from the light. As the figure moved near, it became apparent that the figure was his father. Fred stepped back from the telescope in complete surprise. Questions flooded young Fred's mind. Was he really seeing his father? Were his tired eyes playing tricks on him? Dare he look through the lens of the telescope again, for fear of disappointment? Where in his scientific journals had he read about this? Astrological folklore was one thing, but this was something else.

At long last, he garnered the fortitude to look through the lens. No sooner had he pressed his eye to the lens than he felt himself overcome by the light. In one direction, he could see his father standing, arm outstretched toward him. In the other direction, he could see the ever-shrinking telescope eyepiece and a spherical fragment of his front porch beyond the curved glass. Fred felt his emotions being lifted from him into the atmospheric vapor all around him. His head lightened as his earthly conceptions fled his present state. Fear, wonder, doubt, and resistance swirled away on a sliver of refulgent nothingness. Gone was gravity, along with any perception of time or direction. The next thing Fred saw was his father's blue-soaked essence next to him. A ripple in the light made his father's head wave in circular streams. At the center of the ripple, Fred saw his mother's face. She smiled the pleasant hollow smile of an unwritten love poem. She waved at Fred over her husband's face—a face he could still clearly see. Fred tried to speak to his mother, but all his words became strange lilting notes wafting across an endless pastel void. Her reply was an echo of oddly floating notes. Her eyes drew him in, and he realized that he was seeing things from her perspective. He found himself looking at himself—not in a mirror, but in the truest present moment.

Things flashed hard inside Fred's head, as if he had been struck over the head by some blunt cosmic instrument. The blue lights' intensity immediately cracked across whatever shapeless space he was now in. He opened his eyes, only to realize he was sprawled out on the front porch beneath his telescope. His head ached as it had never ached before. Slowly, and with great caution, Fred got up. Everything around him seemed normal. The clear night showed off a beautiful, dazzling galaxy against a sharp black sky. The telescope still sat quietly on its tripod, and the furniture on the porch looked like it always had. What had just happened?

Fred went inside to see if his mother was all right, but her door was closed. He knocked gently and asked if she was all right.

A voice from the room answered in oddly floating notes, "Come along dear…."

Fred opened the door, only to find a tidy vacant room. He turned to see the bluish-purple light illuminate the house. He quickly returned to his telescope, still on the front porch. When he got to the porch, he could see the light was illuminating from the eyepiece of the telescope. With great intensity, he grabbed the telescope and pressed his left eye to the end facing him. As the brightness engulfed him, he found himself once again in the presence of his parents.

As Fred approached his father, he noticed that he was wearing a uniform—not the usual ranger uniform he always wore, but a different uniform. The insignia on the uniform's sleeve was foreign to Fred; he did not recognize it. Just as he was about to ask his father what the symbol meant, the space they were in began to turn and twist as if it was being swept away in some ferocious summer storm. When Fred next realized his condition, he was in a suspended state and connected to all sorts of strange instruments. Soon, though, a figure disconnected him and led him down what appeared to be a long hallway and into a queerly colored space. Near him stood his mother and father, but the uniform was gone and both his parents seemed to be nondescriptly naked. They also appeared to be together, as in one in the same. Fred reached out to his family, only to be drawn into them. Fred began to dissipate into them, as they oozed into others and the others were as one light illuminating the heavens.

Allia, Fred's oldest sister, spread out the checkered blanket on the warm dry summer grass and remarked to her husband how bright the stars seemed since she had lost her brother the year before. She remarked that she missed him, and that she had, before his passing, always left the stargazing to him. She knew where he was and that he was watching the same stars that night. Her husband hugged her tightly and affirmed her thoughts about her brother as the two of them stared up to the heavens.

19
The Lincolnshire Hotel

Charlotte, North Carolina, was, in the early 20th Century, known throughout the mid-south as a high-society playground. The nearby Appalachian Mountains provided year round skiing, hiking, rafting, leaf peeping, and partying.

Upon its completion, in 1904, the Lincolnshire Hotel was the center of social life in Charlotte. Guests from as far away as Washington, D.C. and Pittsburgh flocked to its magnificent opulence. The Lincolnshire Hotel, in its day, was considered a high rise of the new American era. With many rooms and much entertainment space, the Lincolnshire was an undeniable hot spot. Society parties were regular events attended by locals and weekenders alike.

The Lincolnshire Hotel was buzzing with Christmas and end of the Great War celebrations in late November, 1918. Hallways and foyers were strewn with White Pine garlands and enormous wreaths. A swing band played the latest arrangements to crowds of swirling partygoers. Champagne flowed like liquid joy and the banquet table was overstocked with meats and desserts. The hotel's rooms were full and the ballroom was filled endlessly

Haunted Charlotte

This building, along Tryon Street, is said to be the former Lincolnshire Hotel.

19: The Lincolnshire Hotel

with happy travelers. The porter moved the luggage from place to place, but he always seemed to be staring around with the suspicion of an escaped convict. He did his job, but the manager still distrusted him.

The manager kept a keen eye on all of the guests. Though there were many people coming and going, he knew them all by name or face. Personal greetings were necessary to keep the high-end guests satisfied and the manager was good at his job.

It was at one of these parties in the grand ballroom that the hotel manager first noticed the stranger lurking about the halls. The stranger first caught the manager's attention when he saw the man hovering in the far corner of the second-story interior balcony. He had a full beard and long hair, but he was thin and sickly looking, although he was dressed appropriately for the occasion. The manager began to walk toward the man, but as he approached him, the stranger vanished into the crowd. An hour or so later, the overseer again saw the thin stranger moving weirdly down one of the stairways. He seemed to be at the party alone. He spoke to no one, and no one spoke to him. While maintaining his decorum, the manager moved slyly through the throngs of people in a secret search for the illusive stranger.

Was he planning some sort of ambuscade on the hotel or was he a legitimate guest that had initially escaped the introduction of the manager? The hotel proprietor could not be for sure. One thing, though, was clear to the manager: he needed to find out what the stranger's story was. In order to accomplish this, he would have to find him first. For more than an hour, the manager and the stranger slipped and weaved through the crowded hotel. The labyrinth of people made contact impossible. Whenever the proprietor thought he had caught up to the man, he was gone again. From what the manager could tell, the stranger was not aware of him, or eluding him on purpose. The stranger just seemed to be vanishing and reappearing like the moon on a stormy night.

At last, the midnight hour chimed its deathly knell and the manager walked around a corner straight into the arms of the stranger. No sooner had the stranger and the manager met, than the thin man fell to the floor unconscious. His top hat rolled across the rug in an awkward spin. The overseer called for help. They quickly got the bearded man to one of the only empty beds in the hotel. A doctor in attendance was beckoned to come and evaluate the man. The doctor said that the man needed rest, and that he would come back in the morning to check on him and make further evaluations. The manager ordered the stranger's door locked and a guard set outside of it. With this, the manager sent everyone else away and returned to his own quarters for a restless night's sleep.

Haunted Charlotte

When his alarm clock rattled, long before sunrise, the manager got up, got dressed, and went to check on the previous night's uninvited guest. Questions stirred in his mind as he walked down the main hallway to the stranger's room. When he walked past room 337, the manager caught a glimpse of the porter across the balcony. The porter just glared with a stark, sinister gaze. At the room of the uninvited guest, the manager found the stranger lying in bed—ice-cold dead.

The frustrated manager rang for all the proper authorities to come and conduct the necessary procedures. From the corpse, the hotel executives gathered the stranger's personal items and laid them out neatly on a table. A nondescript silver ring, antique cuffs, wire-rimmed glasses, an expensive cigarette case with a lighter, and a billfold without any identification were the only specialty items among his possessions. The clerk wondered aloud whether the stranger might have been a pickpocket working the crowded hotel. Since no items such as these had been reported missing or stolen the previous evening, the items were cataloged and put in a shoebox. The dead man's possessions were then sent to the basement storage room, in case someone stepped forward to claim them.

The corpse was sent to the city morgue. No one claimed the body and no identification was ever established. As far as the city was concerned, the stranger was just another John Doe. The Charlotte coroner decided the suit he had on was good enough for an anonymous burial and the stranger was sent to be buried in an unmarked grave at the margins of the city lot. The Lincolnshire Hotel manager was the only person in attendance when the plain wooden casket was lowered into the rapidly freezing North Carolina soil. The stranger had weighed heavily on the manager's mind, but he was a pragmatic man and he immediately began to turn his mind back to his responsibilities at the hotel. He had, after all, a large staff and many guests to account for.

The stranger had not been buried long when the staff and guests at the Lincolnshire began to report strange noises around the hotel and its grounds. A waitress reported feeling a hand slipping into her apron pocket when no one was around. Several clients checked out early with complaints about sounds in their quarters. Doors were left open that should have been closed. A gardener claimed to have seen a gravestone appear in the garden, but when the manager went to look, there was no marker at that place. Dishwashers in the kitchen kept finding the sinks clogged with rags.

The manager simply told the staff to get back to work. He scoffed at the complaints being supernatural. Lights flickered for no apparent reason. Horses reared up and snorted as they approached the edifice. Day after day, the workers at the hotel would complain of strange or ghostly goings on, to which the manager would reply that he did not believe in apparitions. He would tell the workers to continue with their assigned tasks and not to bother him again with such nonsense.

The next April, on a cold, rainy day, the manager was working late and needed to retrieve something from the basement storerooms; on his way to the storerooms, he felt that he was being watched by the porter. Down in the dank catacombs, as the manager bent over a crate to unhinge it, a shadow passed over him. The shadow caused the manager to quickly turn and face the impeded light source from over his shoulder. Before him stood a man-shaped shadow. The manager braced himself on the crate, staring in awe at the darkened figure before him.

To the overseer's surprise, the shadow spoke to him in a clear unwavering voice with a strong Ukrainian accent: "I am what remains of Ivan Rashmonikov, the stranger you so distrusted in these very halls in the weeks before the birthday of our Lord and Savior."

The manager swallowed hard, and continued to stare at the thing before him. The shadow continued: "I did not mean to arouse your suspicions; I was only looking for my wife, who was supposed to be in attendance at your festivities. I was working late and told her I would meet her here at the completion of my business week. News came to me that she had never left home to travel here, due to the weather. She must be frantically looking for me in our hometown of Pittsburgh. Please, kind sir, write to her, explain of my passing, and ask her to gather my things and give me a proper burial."

With that, the shadow disappeared into the darkness of the storeroom walls. Nearly shaken into hysteria, the manager climbed out of the basement and returned to his office.

With shaking hands, he opened a bottle of brandy, poured himself a drink, and reached for a fountain pen. He wrote the letter he was instructed to write—a letter to a woman he did not know, a letter dictated to him by a ghost he did not believe in. No sooner had he signed the letter than he passed out on his desk.

He awoke the next morning sore and unsure of the previous night's occurrences. He could scarcely tell whether it had been real, the brandy, or a bad dream. Nevertheless, there before him, was the letter. The manager mailed the letter in secrecy, not wanting to reveal to his staff that he had written such a thing. Besides, he was half expecting it to be returned as undeliverable.

Except for a few unexplainable noises coming up through the floorboards from the basement, the next several weeks at the Lincolnshire went by quietly. The staff had learned that complaints about weird sightings were ignored. Still, though, the porter stared that strange stare. The manager continued to keep a watchful eye on his staff. The tension in the air was as thick as Cincinnati Chili.

It was pushing the end of May when a 1917 Model T pulled up in front of the Hotel. Out stepped an elegantly dressed woman. She walked with poise and dignity up to the front desk clerk and asked to see the manager. Once seated in the manager's office with a hot cup of coffee in her hands, the manager asked, "What may we do for you?"

The woman replied, "I am Mrs. Ivan Rashmonikov, and I received a letter from you stating that my husband had died at your hotel some weeks before Christmas last. Your letter instructed me to claim his personal effects and mark his grave properly. Am I correct in my understanding of the situation?

Stunned, the manager searched for the right words to assuage the obviously annoyed woman. At last, he simply replied, "Yes ma'am, that is correct." He looked over at his assistant and said, "Bob, please go get Mr. Rashmonikov's personal items from the storerooms."

"Yes sir," replied Bob.

Mrs. Rashmonikov continued, "Is there anything else you can tell me about my husband's death?"

"Well, here is the address for the coroner's office where you may receive a copy of his death certificate and a postmortem report. They may ask you to confirm his identity from a photograph, as I reported his death as a person unknown. I have also written down the location of his grave, so you may visit it, to give your condolences or apply for reburial."

With that, Mrs. Rashmonikov stood up, nodded, and said, "Thank you." After a long pause, she turned back to the manager and asked, "Sir, how did you know to write me…if he was unknown to you?"

"Well, Mrs. Rashmonikov," the manager replied, "I'll never again deny the existence of ghosts."

Mrs. Rashmonikov looked reflectively at the floor before re-affixing her gaze upon the manager. "Neither then, shall I," she replied, as she disappeared behind the office door.

20
Mrs. Aberley

The House of Aberley was built in the spring of 1867 on what was then abandoned rural farmland. The farm was on the site of what was rumored to have been a Union Civil War encampment, less than a day's journey north of the strategically important North Carolina-South Carolina state line. The house was built for the soon-to-be-retired Mr. John Aberley and his wife and, upon its completion, the Aberleys moved into the home.

It was just over five years later, though, that Mr. Aberley died under very mysterious circumstances. He was found in the front foyer nearly drained of blood, yet no marks or wounds of any kind were found on his body. Mrs. Aberley had him buried in the large side yard, near the garden. Upon the reading of his will, it was revealed that he had left the house to Mrs. Aberley. The contents of the will surprised no one. The death of Mr. Aberley left Mrs. Aberley living in the rather large house as a widow, along with a single housekeeper. Mrs. Aberley had the large master bedroom on the second floor, while the housekeeper had a small bedroom just off the kitchen on the first floor.

The next couple of years were difficult for Mrs. Aberley. She and Mr. Aberley had been happily married for many years, and she missed him terribly. One of her sons had been killed fighting for the Union and her other son had moved far away with his new wife. Her only daughter had died in childbirth, along with the baby. Even her estranged ex-son-in-law had fallen into a sad life as a drunk. She often wore black, as she was now in an almost constant state of mourning.

Haunted Charlotte

As the months went by, the housekeeper could hear Mrs. Aberley talking more and more frequently to the ghost of Mr. Aberley. It was clear that Mrs. Aberley was not going to accept that she was a widow; she obviously continued to think of herself as actively married. The housekeeper just smiled sweetly one evening when Mrs. Aberley asked her to set the table for two. Over the next few weeks, Mrs. Aberley began to recount stories of Mr. Aberley in the first person. Things began to get even stranger when Mrs. Aberley asked the housekeeper to set the dining room table for four. Mrs. Aberley said her deceased son, her daughter, and husband would be joining her for dinner. The housekeeper set the table as she was told, knowing all the while she would only need to wash one set of dishes. Mrs. Aberley's strange behavior continued to amuse the housekeeper, who played along to not illicit any anger from her employer.

Then, on the morning of November 21, 1876, Mrs. Aberley woke up early and began to search the house. She went wildly through her desk and continued looking in the chest at the foot of her bed. She then started pacing up and down the upstairs hallway, her shoes pounding on the rugs and clattering on the hardwood floors. The noise of the furious search woke up the housekeeper, who stood in her room listening for several long minutes to the sounds of the frantic search. She could hear Mrs. Aberley upstairs, going noisily through her things. The housekeeper could hear the creaking of the armoire doors as Mrs. Aberley searched through its contents. The oversized door latch made an unusual clattering sound as it was shut. Sounds of scraping on the hardwood floors could be heard from the guest bedroom at the back of the house as furniture was dragged from one end of the room to the other. The housekeeper could hear Mrs. Aberley angrily mumbling to herself from across the hallway. She was not sure whether to interrupt her or just leave well enough alone. With nervous curiosity, the housekeeper listened to the slamming of the desk drawers in the parlor and the swishing of the drapes at the front windows. Mrs. Aberley was roaming around the house as someone lost in a maze.

When the housekeeper could no longer restrain herself from her own curiosity, she went to Mrs. Aberley and asked, "Dear, is there anything I can help you with; is there anything I can help you find?"

Mrs. Aberley spun around and shrieked, "I cannot find it, I cannot find it, I cannot find it!"

That was Mrs. Aberley's only reply to the question. She then turned her attention back to the furious search. She stormed off to the attic to leave the housekeeper standing in the hallway feeling confused. Creepy irregular sounds began to emanate from the attic as Mrs. Aberley continued to search through crates and chests. The attic had accumulated several years' worth

20: Mrs. Aberley

Is Mrs. Aberley home?

of trunks and bundles. There was a lot to go through in the attic, and Mrs. Aberley was up there seeking for more than two hours. The housekeeper retreated to the kitchen, where she continued to listen to the sounds of the search, yet she did not know what Mrs. Aberley was searching for. The search continued for hours—each passing hour more painful than the last.

Eventually, the midnight hour rolled around and the house of Aberley at last became silent. After hours of creaking, slamming, and scraping, an oddly morose mood settled over the house like a blanket of darkness. It was nearly one in the morning when the housekeeper finally went to bed, only to have a restless night. Not knowing what Mrs. Aberley was searching for led to tense dreams of ceaseless longing and she could not get Mrs. Aberley's weird, uncharacteristic behavior out of her mind. She awoke early in the morning to take Mrs. Aberley her breakfast in bed, only to find her in her bed, ice-cold dead. The housekeeper rang for the mortuary and the body was taken and prepared for burial next to Mr. Aberley in the side-yard gravesite. Her funeral was held at the local chapel, but the only two people in attendance, besides the pastor, were the unsober ex-son-in law and the housekeeper. On a freezing January day, she was laid to final rest next to Mr. Aberley.

Haunted Charlotte

Mrs. Aberley's surviving son, John Jr., and his wife Abigail, moved back into the house not long after his mother's burial. The mood in the house of Aberley was always dampened by the sadness of its unfolding history, but Mrs. Aberley's son tried to make the best of the situation. In November of their first year in the house, John Aberley and his wife were expecting their first child. On November 21st, John was awoken early to the sounds of desk drawers slamming shut. It sounded like someone was going through the desk in the parlor. John looked over at his sleeping wife and thought, *It couldn't be her, and no one else should be in the house.* He thought it might be an intruder, and so he got up, put on a bathrobe, and went to investigate. From the head of the stairs, he could only see shadows in the parlor. As John continued to let his eyes adjust to the faint light, nothing else stirred in the house. Back in bed, he listened to the sounds as they began to creep into the bedroom. The clock on the mantle said 5:58; it was nearly time to get up anyway.

All day through, John and Abigail listened to the sounds of the furious search as the ghost of his mother continued looking through the crates in the cellar and hatboxes in the downstairs closet. They sat in the kitchen, hand-in-hand, nervously waiting for the sounds to cease. It was not until midnight that the sounds of the search finally subsided, leaving John and Abigail with frayed nerves and little sleep.

Abigail wrote, some years later, in a journal that every November 21st was the same in the Aberley house. On that date, she and John experienced the sounds of the search with unrelenting terror. They had come to expect the noisy haunting on November 21st, but each year it still filled them with dread.

Several generations of Aberleys lived in that house in the years after John and Abigail, and all those generations reported the sounds of the furious search on the anniversary of November 21st. The creaking of the armoire doors and the scuffing of Mrs. Aberley's feet in the hallway echoed throughout the next century. Still, no successive generation learned what it was that Mrs. Aberley was searching for—the object of the search remained a family mystery.

Then, in December 2007, Tom Aberley, a great-great-great-great grandnephew of Mrs. Aberley, moved into the house. Long before he moved in, though, he was told stories of its ghostly ramblings on November 21st. Tom was well versed in the family's haunted history, for the ghost of Mrs. Aberley was not the only unexplained tale surrounding the Aberley family. He moved in with the confidence that it was only a legend. On his first November 21st, though, Tom found out the legend was true. On that day, he awoke to the sound of creaking attic stairs. With keen interest, he listened

20: Mrs. Aberley

all day to the noises of someone opening and closing chests and closets. Hour after hour, Tom was both frightened and thrilled by the shuffling of feet and the scraping of furniture on the hardwood floors. Tom had no other explanation for the sounds, but was enraptured to be embroiled in the family legend.

The next year, he began to do some remodeling and updating. As part of the work, he opened up a large section of wall, and out fell an old bundle of papers…a *very* old bundle of papers. It was Mrs. Aberley's unfinished will. A will? Was this what Mrs. Aberley had been looking for? A will? Had she had a premonition of her own death? Had she needed this document, to sign it, before her own death? Had the ghost of Mrs. Aberley been searching through the house all these years in search of her will?

Tom is, of course, not sure that this is what the ghost of Mrs. Aberley has been searching for, but he thinks it might be. He claims it might be. He is waiting for November 21st to come, to see if at last the house of Aberley falls silent. He is waiting to see if the ghost of Mrs. Aberley has finally been assuaged. Tom is waiting…Tom is still waiting.

21
A Resentment

The result of resentment.

Resentment is a form of haunting more terrifying than what any ghost can wrought upon one's self.

Resentment is a demon with the patience of a saint.

It casts its spell in the fullness of daylight, in the sliver of the candle's glow, and in the deepest darkness of the soul.

Beware, not of the spectral figure that lurks behind doorways, but of that which remains of your own resentments.

Those ghosts of the past that linger in the shadows of your mind, for they will drive you mad all the sooner and more completely.

—Roy Heizer

22

The Corpses

William O'Landerson was a lawyer who worked all over southern North Carolina. He and his family lived in Charlotte, but he spent a lot of time on the road, traveling from client to client, courthouse to courthouse. On this day, he had spent several hours in the Raleigh courthouse pleading before a judge. He knew he could not make it all the way back to town that night. The darkness of night had already set in and a terrible storm was fast approaching from the southwest. The town of Charlotte was still at least ten miles further down the road. As the storm began to spill its wrath upon William O'Landerson and his horse, he hunched deeper into his saddle, pressing his knees against the warm, wet fenders. He winced in pain as the stinging rain continuously stabbed his back. The rolling hills of south central North Carolina were beginning to look more like some strange foreign land of endless storms than any place William had ever called home. The quarter-lit sky spelled ominous things to come.

Suddenly, in the light of a violent flash of lightning, William caught a glimpse of an old, long-abandoned house down a long, muddy wagon path. He thought he might have seen it before, but he was tired and could not be sure. It had stood empty for years, weather and time clawing at its roof and foundation until the uneven walls leaned at strange angles. The once-grand chimney had been damaged by storms, and little boys playing with rocks had broken out some of the windows. The grounds around the old farmhouse were just as eerie as the house itself. The gnarled, old trees cast creepy shadows across the yard in the moonlight. A half-dilapidated shed in the back of the main house had a loose door that banged constantly in

Though it has never been found, this southern farmhouse is what the house in the story may have looked like at the time.

the wind. What remained of a horse paddy filled out the home's neglected storyline.

However, on this particular April evening, in 1859, the neglected abode was a sanctuary for a weary traveler. He would tie up here for a while, then head on into town when the storm had passed. After all, he'd slept in worse places. As he approached the house, he thought about his wife, waiting for him at home in Charlotte. She would not worry, he thought; she would know he had taken shelter from the weather.

William rode arduously up to the house, tethered his horse to an oak tree in the yard, and made his way to the front door of the farmhouse. William was always a polite man, and even though he was sure the property was long vacant, he knocked to make sure no one was there. Though cold and soaked to the bone, he waited on the splintered, wood porch for a reply. When no one answered the door, he proceeded with his original intent. When William pressed against the heavy wooden door, it would not budge. He had to utilize his last ounce of strength to get it to open. Once inside, he looked at his wet clothes clinging to his body, rainwater running into pools at his feet. He stood in the foyer still able to feel the rain in his riding boots. As he looked around, it was obvious that the house had been empty for quite some time.

Out of exhaustion, he sat on the stairs, put his face in his hands, and shut his eyes for a few minutes of rest. His back and legs ached from the

22: The Corpses

long ride back from Raleigh. He thought to himself, *When I was a young man with a fast and sure-footed Quarter horse, I could have made it home to Charlotte tonight.* However, William was no longer in his youth, and he knew enough to respect his own limitations. He and his horse were tired and they both needed a good, long rest. When William had finally recuperated a bit and opened his weary eyes, he became overwhelmed with a sense that he was not alone in the house. He listened carefully, only to hear the storm still raging outside the windows. He could not hear a sound from inside the house. William stood up and squinted into the dark abyss of the rooms. He could not see anything in the absence of light. Cautiously, he walked from the foyer into the living room. William stared into the large room, but saw only blackness.

    Suddenly, an intense moaning sound assaulted his ears. Was someone sleeping in an upstairs bedroom? If he was alone in the house, what made the noise? Was it the storm? He thought to himself that he had been alone on the road, and his was the only horse tethered at the house.

    Then, suddenly, a flash of lightning lit the living room, and William saw clearly the source of the moaning. Before him stood five hideous corpses, facing him in the momentary light of the lightning. The five corpses were quite degraded, yet bits of putrid flesh still hung off their exposed bones. He gasped as he saw maggots squirming around inside the third corpses left eye socket. William let out a scream that would have awoken the dead if they had not already been standing before him. Who were they? What had happened to them? Were they a father, mother, and three siblings? William felt a warm sensation running down his legs, and he knew it was not the rain. He raised his arm up over his eyes to hide the gruesome sight. When William dared to look again, the bony fingers of accusation were pointing at him. They moved toward William like ground beef oozing through a hand-cranked grinder. At that moment, one of the corpses reached around behind its neck and pulled a gluttonous rat from off its shoulder blade. Their feet lumbered along across the floor, unable to walk correctly without the muscles they once had. William thought he saw exposed blood vessels swaying from a nasty cut to one of the corpse's throat. Nine arms and a bloody stub reached out for William as he doubled over, his stomach turning in wrenching pain and a sickening dizziness coming over him; he passed out.

    When he regained consciousness, he was lying in the soaking, wet grass halfway between the door of the house and the tree where he had tied the horse. The moon had emerged from its hiding place behind the dark storm clouds. The land was as clear and bright as newly shined crystal. Glorious heavenly stars were scattered like diamonds across the North Carolina sky.

Haunted Charlotte

Are you being followed by the Corpses?

No sooner had William gotten his eyes fully opened, than he saw five ghostly figures looming over him.

The ghostly figures said in a strangely unified voice, "Help us! We are stuck between this world and beyond…Find our murderer, bring him to justice, bury our bodies, and give us our last rites."

William's head began to swim. Was he in some unexplainable nightmare? Was this real, or only his exhausted mind coping with its fear. Murders? Murders near Charlotte? He had never heard of such a story. William passed out again, only to awaken later in the wee hours of the morning. Upon his awakening, the sky was clear and he was infinitely alone.

When William related the story the next day, his fellow villagers were disgusted, horrified, and intrigued. For days afterward, they gossiped of nothing else. They speculated endlessly about the identities of the corpses. Who were they? Were they the remains of murdered itinerant farmers? Were they the victims of a robbery gone bad? Did they even exist at all outside of William O'Landerson's imagination? No one knew.

William, for his part, never spoke of that night ever again. Oddly, no one in Charlotte could remember an abandoned farmhouse along the road to Raleigh, but the countryside was wide open in those days and someone might have built a house that had since been forgotten. Several of the local men, at the urging of their wives, mounted up a search brigade and set out to find the abandoned farmhouse. They wanted to investigate the story William had told of corpses and their ghosts on a stormy night. They set out on a cold Saturday morning. No abandoned farmhouse was ever found, but then again… neither was the search party.

23
Elderberry

Lurking in shadowy understory and dark forests, the Elderberry came to be regarded as having supernatural associations. In Northern Europe, it was said to be possessed of a spirit, and no one could destroy it without peril to himself.

Its name associates it with Hulda, or Hilda, mother of elves, the good woman in Northern myth. In Denmark, Hulda lived in the root of the Elder, hence the shrub was her symbol, and was used during the ritual ceremonies of her worship.

It was forbidden to use Elderberry wood in the construction of houses. It was said that the occupant of such a house would feel the pulling of the spirits in his legs, a nasty sensation that could only be relieved by planting three Elderberry shrubs in the forest and assuring their life until maturity and flowering.

Incidentally, Elder wood cures toothaches, fends off snakes, mosquitoes, and warts. It quiets nerves and interrupts fits of madness, removes poison from metal pitchers, keeps fleas out of furniture, makes the home safe, and guarantees he who cultivates it shall die in his own house. While the large white Elderberry flowers were said to represent the purity and brightness of enlightenment, its black berries were gobbled up by all manner of nymphs, fairies, trolls, and warlocks.

Along with all these wonderfully enchanting myths from Europe, Elderberry is also native to the Eastern United States, making it a valuable addition to any native garden. As a large flowering shrub, Elderberry is a

The mysterious Elderberry plant.

standout among its peers. Elderberry wine has long been a traditional drink in many cultures, and is known to be a witch's potion.

The Elderberry can be found growing wild throughout Mecklenburg County.

24
Aunt Sally

Little is known about the life of young Sally Johnson, only that she was born in Mecklenburg County, North Carolina, in 1896, and that she lived a short, happy life along the banks of Lake Norman with her sister, Maude, and her three brothers, William, Delbert, and Brady. While little about her life is on record, her tragic death haunts Lake Norman near her hometown of Davidson, North Carolina.

In 1909, Davidson, North Carolina, was a small struggling lakeside town, not unlike hundreds of others along the lakes, rivers, and waterways of the south. Life was simpler in those days, and children were free to play around town without parental concern for strangers or tragedy. Mr. and Mrs. Johnson were not at all concerned when, one hot summer day, William, Delbert, Brady, and Sally wanted to go play down at the lake. William was sixteen and a responsible young man who had watched out for his younger siblings several times before. With Brady, Delbert, and Sally in tow, William set off for an adventure on the lake. Maude stayed at home to play with her dolls.

The four of them got to the lake at ten in the morning and began to play "Hide and Go Seek" around the docks and piers. First Brady, then William, took turns hiding among the crates, barrels, and boats along the lake bank. For more than an hour they played, laughing and romping with each other. As the game went on though, new places to hide got scarcer, and each child had begun to get more and more creative in their choice of hiding places.

A little after 11 a.m., it was William's turn to seek and, upon a raucous "ready or not, here I come," William set off to look for his brothers and sister among the boats and fishing sheds. He searched and searched and searched; time drew out and he began to get just a little nervous. Finally, though, he found Brady and Delbert hiding quietly behind a stack of firewood down near Old Man Dorsonette's out building. Brady belted out a hearty laugh at how long it had taken William to find him, but William was not amused. He was getting worried that he had not yet found Sally. The three boys went off in search of their sister. They searched for Sally through every shed and along every dock. They pushed over every barrel they could, they looked under and in every wagon on the lake bank, but to no avail. They could not find Sally anywhere. The younger boy who still thought this was all a game, laughed at how clever his sister had been in picking a hiding place. William had realized that they were no longer playing a game, but he wanted to keep Brady and Delbert calm and so he continued to tell them they were still having fun looking for Sally.

After more than an hour, William finally decided it was time for help. While working to keep Brady preoccupied, William told several people that he and his siblings were playing a game of "Hide and Go Seek," and could they tell him if they had seen young Sally hiding anywhere. The answer was always, "No, I haven't seen Sally today." William and Brady kept searching, but without a resolution.

It was when William was about to give up and go home to get his parents, that he heard a shriek that pierced the summer air. It was the kind of scream one was not likely to forget. William's blood turned cold at the sound, and he turned and took Brady's hand. The young boys headed down to the lake's edge where the scream had come from. The three boys were quickly joined by several older men who had been working or fishing along the nearby water. A crowd quickly gathered, but William pushed his way to the front of the crowd, only to see Sally's lifeless body floating face down in the water. William wailed, while Brady just stood there, staring over at a horse that was nearby.

A man reached over, touched Brady on the shoulder, and said, "Hey boy, what are you staring at?"

Brady just kept staring at the horse and saying the word "Kelpie" repeatedly. Several of the men had to hold William back from diving into the water.

"I will get Mr. Johnson," said one of the fishermen sadly. "He will want to pull her out, and he will need our help."

As he choked back tears, Sally's father pulled her from the lake. Mrs. Johnson stood on the dock and wept inconsolably while several of the local

24: Aunt Sally

women tried to comfort her. Sally had drowned while trying to hide in the water. She had submerged herself to, apparently, get under one of the fishing boats. A loose nail on the bottom of the boat caught her hair, holding her head underwater.

The Johnsons were devastated, and while Mr. and Mrs. Johnson mourned the loss of their daughter, William took it hardest of all. He blamed himself for not watching her more closely. The townsfolk all felt a sense of loss, for she had embodied Davidson's future.

A funeral was conducted at the church three days later. Almost the entire town of Davidson, North Carolina, came out to pay their respects. At the conclusion of the service, Sally Johnson was laid to rest in the Davidson graveyard. Mr. Johnson was a woodworker and he handmade his daughter's marker out of a good strong piece of oak. He worked for several days carving and polishing it. He must have thought of it as a way of coping with the death of his oldest daughter. William, though no one ever blamed him, fell into a deep depression. Some around town say he never came out from under a cloud of melancholy. Delbert, who had always been a quiet child, became even more withdrawn. Brady was too young at the time to understand fully what had happened, but he later expressed sadness at the loss of his sister. When asked about the horse, Brady denied seeing any horse that fateful day.

The remainder of the Johnson family seemed to carry a cloud over them from then on. The small town, too, seemed a bit darker in the wake of Sally's death. In time, though, things began to get back to something like normal. A few years later, William turned twenty and moved away, never to return to Davidson. Delbert followed William to Winston-Salem, and he, too, never returned to his hometown. After a short apprenticeship with his father, Brady moved away to join a woodworking company. Unlike his brothers, he did return to Davidson every year to visit his parents who, despite their loss, had decided to stay in Davidson in their older years.

By the 1920s, Brady, in a secure job with a profitable company, had gotten married and had a couple of children of his own. Therefore, in the early summer of 1921, he and his wife, Linda, brought their two girls to visit with their grandparents for Memorial Day weekend. Tansy was four that year and Betony had just turned three years old on February 20, 1921. The mood in the family had lightened in recent years and Mrs. Johnson had mostly come to terms with the death of her daughter. The visit was comfortable and relaxing. Brady and his dad spent their time repairing a rock wall and making woodcarvings, while the woman watched the children and conversed about all manner of things great and small.

133

A Johnson family portrait. Young Sally is on the left.

The family visited Sally's grave on Memorial Day, Monday, May 30. They paid their respects and left fresh flowers. Brady and Linda planned to stay for three days, but the elder Johnsons convinced them to stay a few days longer, and so, on June 1, the whole Johnson family packed a picnic lunch and went down to sit by the lake to watch the sailboats pass.

Although the mood was jovial, Mrs. Johnson rarely took her eyes off the two grandchildren, and the younger Johnsons were extra vigilant as the children were playing near the lake. While the adults talked, Betony sat on the edge of the picnic blanket and watched Tansy and some other children playing closer to the docks. Tansy and the other children were deeply engrossed in a game of Tag when the elder Mrs. Johnson called out that it was time to eat.

"Tansy," Mrs. Johnson called, "please, come have lunch."

Tansy looked up from the game of Tag when she heard her grandmother's voice, and came running over to where the adults were.

"Granma," said Tansy, "can my new friend come to share lunch with us too?"

Mrs. Johnson looked up from her plate and, seeing no one with Tansy, said, "Why, yes dear, if it's all right with her parents, you may go and get her."

24: Aunt Sally

Tansy looked puzzled, and then said very matter-of-factly, "But Granma, she's right here, can't you see her? She says her name is Sally."

At that moment, Betony got up from the picnic blanket and ran over to the little girl standing next to Tansy. Betony said to the little girl, "Have you come to play with us?" Betony continued, "You look like my sister, Tansy, are you friends?"

All four of the adult Johnsons were stunned, for they could see no one standing there except Tansy and Betony. The adults looked first at each other, for answers or confirmation, or anything. The younger Mrs. Johnson was the first to speak, saying, "Tansy, are you sure your friend is here?"

"Yes Mommy," said Tansy.

After a long silence, Mrs. Johnson said, "Tansy, you said her name was Sally…did she tell you that?"

"Yes, Mommy," said Tansy. "She told me that down by the edge of the water. She said her name was Sally and that she had been playing "Hide and Go Seek" with her brothers, but they never found her."

The elder Mrs. Johnson, at that moment, broke down and began wailing as if she were bereft of all joy.

The elder Mr. Johnson hugged his wife and said to his granddaughter, "Tansy, how do know that?"

Tansy just stared at her grandfather as if the answer was obvious. Brady Johnson had a worried look on his face as a flood of memories came back into his mind. The memories of that fateful family day nearly overcame him, and he fell into a restless dream-like state.

Tansy turned to look at the little girl standing next to her and asked, "Do you like sugar in your tea?"

Meanwhile, Betony continued to pull on the seam of the apparitional Sally's dress.

The adults were upset. Clearly, the children saw someone they did not. Were they in the presence of a ghost? Could it be that young Sally Johnson had come back from the dead to play with her nieces? Could it be that their beloved Sally was alive in some form after all? Did the children really see Sally? Or, were they merely playing along with some story they had overheard? The questions swirled through the adults and they became ensnared in their own frantic wonderment.

The younger Mrs. Johnson, having only heard the story of Sally, was the least connected to the memories of her tragedy. She was, therefore, the first of the adults to get herself pulled together. There was no use in upsetting the children. She reassured the other adults that this sort of thing was normal and that they should just play along with it.

The adults that day kept an awkward silence as they ate their picnic lunch and watched Tansy and Betony play with the ghost of their Aunt Sally. After lunch, Tansy asked if the other two girls and she could go and play with the other children near the lake. The elder Mrs. Johnson looked worried, not knowing how to answer.

Brady then looked up at his mother, "Mother," he said, "I think it will be all right. Their Aunt Sally will protect them."

Brady's mother looked down at him and replied with tears in her eyes, "Yes, dear, I'm sure your right."

Tansy, Betony, and Aunt Sally skipped down to the banks of Lake Norman to play with the other children. The adults watched while the other children seemed to play with Sally and the two girls as if nothing was strange.

Over the next seven years, until she was twelve years old, Tansy talked about playing with Sally near the lake when she came to visit her grandparents. In the summer of her thirteenth year, Tansy made no mention of Sally to her parents or grandparents. From that summer on, in fact, Sally floated off into Tansy's memories. Betony also never mentioned Sally again after her thirteenth birthday.

In the years since 1921, the other children of Davidson have from time to time reported seeing the ghostly figure of a young girl down by the lake's shore near the docks. Some have reported interacting with her, while others have said they simply saw her playing among the docks and fishing sheds. No child, however, over the age of twelve has ever claimed to have seen her. Local legend has it that Sally is forever playing along the shores of Lake Norman with the children of Davidson, North Carolina.

25
The Old Elmwood Cemetery

The Old Elmwood Cemetery holds many ghostly tales. George Samuel Heizer, a relative of the author of this book, who is buried here, is said to haunt the Cemetery.

Haunted Charlotte

Located near uptown Charlotte, the Elmwood Cemetery graces the gentle hills just west of the central business district. The views of Charlotte from the cemetery are the very definition of bucolic—but do not let the magnificent views fool you into thinking that all those that reside there stay within their legendary tombs.

A visitor may stroll the winding roads, but they to be aware that they are not alone. Among others, a man by the name of George S. Heizer wanders these hauntingly beautiful hills. A relative of the author of these stories, George S. Heizer presents a ghostly shadow to many who visit here. As one glides along the paths beside the markers, he may well introduce himself and ask them if they intend on joining him there some day.

As his closest living relative, I can assure you he is harmless. He is simply a southern gentleman showing hospitality to those seeking solace among the hills of Elmwood Cemetery.

Bodies and mysteries are entombed in the Old Elmwood Cemetery.

25: The Old Elmwood Cemetery

New skyscrapers and old skyscrapers intertwine in Charlotte's haunted history.

26
The Playmate

Most young children have an imaginary friend at some point in their childhood. Some children "bring to life" a stuffed animal or toy, while others have wholly self-conceived human friends. This imaginary friend is someone who they can play with when and how they wish. Most parents and psychologists feel that, within reason, this is a harmless and sometimes a fruitful stage of development. When carefully supervised, playing with an imaginary friend, or animated toy, can help a child develop empathy, manners, or good sportsmanship. At the very least, it helps many children cope with being alone and keeps them out of trouble. For most children, the imaginary friend stage lasts between two and five years, resulting in no long-term harm.

Anna Leigh Wellper's mother, Joyce, had found the almost-new stuffed bear at a neighbor's garage sale. She gave the bear to Anna Leigh the afternoon she found it. It was a thank-you-for-behaving-while-I-was-shopping gift. The little girl took to the bear right away and Anna Leigh's parents thought that their daughter's large, stuffed bear made a cute imaginary friend.

Anna Leigh played with the bear night and day for several weeks. Her mother noticed that she had developed quite a bond with the stuffed animal she had named Arnold. Joyce could hear Anna Leigh in her room carrying on long conversations with Arnold. From time to time, Anna Leigh would claim that Arnold had moved something that was not in its right place, or not hung up her coat as he had promised to do. Joyce would laugh to herself over these funny occurrences, but she would never let Anna Leigh off the

26: The Playmate

hook for misbehavior. At other times, Joyce could hardly get Arnold out of her daughter's hands long enough to eat dinner. Sometimes, Anna Leigh would say that Arnold had done something, and then admit that it had been her all along. The two of them, Anna Leigh and Arnold, were becoming the best of friends.

Neither Joyce nor her husband, Felix, felt that Anna Leigh was out of balance over Arnold. She played with the other children in daycare and at church without any irregularities. In fact, Anna Leigh willingly shared Arnold with the other children at church. The bond between Anna Leigh and Arnold was so strong that Joyce was not surprised when her daughter turned down getting a real-life puppy in favor of keeping Arnold. Life with Arnold continued in the Wellper house without a major incident until the fall of 1952.

On a chilly November day, Joyce decided that she wanted to take Anna Leigh for a walk around the neighborhood. Joyce and her daughter almost never took walks together and she had told Anna Leigh that this outing would be special. She bundled up, put on two pairs of socks, and got out the stroller that Anna Leigh was about to outgrow. With Anna Leigh dressed for the weather and Arnold in tow, the two set off on their walk. When they had gotten a few blocks down the street, Anna Leigh loudly proclaimed that Arnold had just told her that they were in front of the house where he had killed his previous owner. Joyce was shocked at her daughter's proclamation. She knew that small children sometimes said outrageous things, but this was clearly the strangest thing Anna Leigh had ever said. Joyce just stared at the house they were in front of, overcome by a sense of Déjà vu. She tried her best not to play into the comments, turned the stroller around, and headed back home. She vaguely remembered that there had been rumors around the neighborhood a few years prior about a child who had been murdered, but Joyce could not remember if it was true or just gossip.

Upon arriving back at their house, Joyce put Anna Leigh in her room and went downstairs to phone Felix. The Wellpers spent the rest of the evening contemplating their daughter's bizarre comments. They made all sorts of excuses to themselves. They settled on: "Maybe I just misheard or misunderstood her comments," and let it go at that. Joyce did not sleep well that night.

The following morning strange things involving Anna Leigh and Arnold began to happen around the Wellper house. Felix was up early going through his usual morning routine, when he heard a scream from Anna Leigh's room. He ran to the room as fast as he could, shouting for Joyce to join him. He burst into the room only to find his daughter fast asleep in her bed with

Arnold curled up around her. As he turned to leave the room, he thought he caught a glimpse of Arnold winking a malicious wink at him. Now it was, he thought, his turn to be taken aback by the large, stuffed bear. The couple hugged in the hallway and agreed to talk about the bear when he returned home from work that evening.

That night, Joyce and Felix went over the strange things that had recently happened with the bear. They agreed that everything had been fine until Anna Leigh had gotten Arnold. They decided to keep an eye on the relationship between their daughter's behavior and Arnold. Felix thought that all kids go through phases, but Joyce was concerned.

Joyce was cleaning up the kitchen the next day, when she realized that one of her knives was missing. She went looking for it, only to find it under Arnold in Anna Leigh's room. She was on the verge of throwing Arnold out, but Felix convinced her that it could not have been Arnold that had taken it.

At lunch a couple days later, Anna Leigh was getting fussy about her vegetables, and Joyce was trying to be patient with her. In a fit of childish rage, Anna Leigh shouted out, "If you make me eat this, I'll get Arnold to kill you, too!"

Joyce was nearly beside herself at the crazy threat Anna Leigh had just made. "You know what, little girl, you are going to lose that bear if I hear one more word about him killing!"

The two of them had a shouting match that left both of them upset at themselves and with each other. Joyce sent Anna Leigh to her room, and she fell exhausted onto the couch. Joyce fell into a restless half sleep. About an hour later, she was awoken to the sound of Anna Leigh's voice.

"I'm sorry, Mommy. I'm sorry." Mother and daughter hugged and all was forgiven.

Though everything was all right, Joyce was still a bit rattled. That evening, when Felix got home, Joyce told him she was going out for a walk, that she just needed some time alone.

"I'll watch Anna Leigh," Felix told her.

"Can you be a big girl and behave for daddy while I go out for a bit?"

"Yes, Mommy."

With that, Joyce put on her heavy overcoat and gloves.

The late November air brought uncomfortably chilly winds and the smell of turkey to Joyce's senses. She pulled her coat collar closer and smiled at the scent of potpourri and pumpkin. Before long, she found herself standing in front of the house where Anna Leigh had made that strange comment a few days earlier. Her listless gaze was broken by the sound of a friendly voice.

26: The Playmate

Arnold.

"Happy Thanksgiving neighbor!" the friendly looking woman sitting on the front porch said.

The woman was nearly hidden by the darkness and the holiday decorations that surrounded her. "Fine brisk evening for a walk," she said.

"Oh, yes, it is," replied a somewhat stunned Joyce.

"Would you like to join me for a cup of hot cider?" the neighbor asked.

Joyce thought about it for a second and then said, "Sure," joining the woman on her front porch.

"What is your name?" Joyce asked the woman.

"Carol...as in Christmas Carol," the woman, replied.

The two women talked for what seemed to Joyce to be a long time. Eventually, after she became a bit more comfortable with Carol, Joyce mentioned Anna Leigh's comment. No sooner had the remark come out of Joyce's mouth, than she realized why she had had such a strong sense of Déjà vu at Carol's house. This was the house where she had gotten the stuffed bear for Anna Leigh back in the spring. Carol was the one who had held the garage sale. Joyce's head began to spin and she felt sick to her stomach. Carol had sold her the bear. Losing all self-control, Joyce spilled the story of Arnold all over Carol. She begged Carol, with tears flowing down her face, to tell her about the bear. Where had it come from, what was its backstory? Joyce had been so wrapped up in her own world that she had not noticed that Carol was also falling into a deep state of depression.

It turned out that Carol had bought the bear for her own daughter the Christmas before. Hailey had wanted a stuffed bear badly, and so Carol had gotten her one. No sooner had Hailey received her bear, than the two fell madly into their own world of imagination. Things took a bizarre turn when Hailey began to blame the bear for all sorts of frightening episodes. Carol told Joyce that she was about to get rid of the bear when she came home one night in February to find her husband and her daughter lying in the backyard. Their blood had seeped into the snow and frozen into the icy crystals. The only evidence the police ever found was fake animal hair on the handle of the knife. The same type of fake fur that was found on the knife handle was also covering the bear. She said to Joyce that she had not destroyed the bear because, of course, it was ridiculous to think that the bear was responsible. Carol claimed that she held the garage sale to rid herself of the things she associated with her husband and daughter, as a way of healing.

Carol looked up to see Joyce running wildly down the street toward her house, running as if she was being chased by the devil.

27
Rosedale Plantation

I began to keep a journal not long after I came into the employ of Dr. Caldwell at The Rosedale Plantation. The Doctor hired me as a gardener and for general laborer about twenty years ago, in the early spring of 1840. It was to be my main employment to tend the plantation's rather extensive gardens. The builder and original owner of Rosedale, an Archibald Frew, had built the house in 1815, and started the gardens and landcrafting several years prior to my arrival. Dr. Caldwell and his wife were now expanding the gardens around the grounds. He had come, as I remember, into proprietorship of the plantation after the original owner passed into the spirit world. The house itself, simply called Rosedale, was rather ample for its day, and the second story of the Federal Style clapboard house sat high up off the ground and looked down over the sloping lawn, which totaled just over 900 acres.

When I began to see odd things around the grounds, I thought that writing down the particulars would be the best course to take. Lest anyone think me mad, I began to keep a journal to document the supernatural happenings around the plantation. It all started on a rather dull day in the fall of 1841, the kind of day uninterrupted by sunshine. I had just finished planting a great number of Boxwood shrubs that Dr. Caldwell had recently imported from England especially for his collection. I sat down on a stump near the edge of the clearing and surveyed the vast countryside laid out

The house at Rosedale Plantation.

before me. That was the first time I saw him. I say first, only to imply it happened again. Here, look for yourself at a portion of the entries in the Journal.

Journal Entry for Tuesday, November 2, 1841
Having had the prior owner of this Rosedale plantation near Charlotte, in the state of North Carolina, described to me, I recognized him almost immediately: short, stout, and well dressed. I saw him this day out on the bowling green...except when he had previously been described to me, I was told that he had died prior to my current employment by Dr. Caldwell. I was of heightened sensibilities about what might be generously described as "A Ghost."

Here before me, standing on the lawn, was the man earlier described to me as Archibald Frew. He was a short, pudgy man as round as he was tall. He was dressed as a gentleman farmer, neat and orderly, but plain. He wore nickers and leg stockings, a common white shirt, and a brown vest with three shiny silver buttons. His hands were clean, but rough from working the handle of a rake or shovel. His hair was neatly combed into a clump at the back of his head, and secured there by a ribbon of cloth.

I have decided to write down this experience here, but keep it verbally to myself. Having not spoken at length with Dr. Caldwell, I do not know

27: Rosedale Plantation

where his religious beliefs lay beyond the door of Shegaw Creek Presbyterian Church, where he goes each Sunday in the morning hours. I do not want to create an issue with my employment over the sighting of a spirit, for it may, in all reality, have been a figment of a tired mind at the end of a long day's labor.

Journal Entry for Monday, November 29, 1841
I again today saw, but kept to myself, the ghostly figure of Archibald Frew, the prior owner of this property called Rosedale Plantation. This time it happened as I worked to clear the ground near the barn. I was standing at the edge of the stable when I looked up from my labors to see a shadow pass the doorframe. It was not ordinary shadow, as if from some limb or passing bird. It was the shadow of Archibald Frew from the other side of the eternal curtain.

Journal Entry for Thursday, December 23, 1841
On this day, Thursday, before the Merriment of the Christmas season, the snow is light upon the fence rails and a thin layer of ice covers the wellhead. A stray flake of snow falls from the dark cloud-laden sky. Christmas festivities are all around the plantation. The heavenly scent of freshly baked bread rose up from the ovens in the cellar, and freshly cut herbs blended their flavors to the sweet smell of sugar plum pies in the kitchen. Everyone, including the staff, is in the throes of merry making.

    I stood, just over an hour ago, in the hall doorway looking into the living room, and that is when, for the Christmas season, Archibald Frew appeared to me. He was hiding merrily behind the tree that was draped in garlands of popcorn. Being nearly as wide as the tree, I could barely make out the happy figure behind the celebrations centerpiece. His shiny metal tin cup reflected the light from the candles. I moved to the center of the room to get a better view, but when I arrived at my new station, the apparition had vanished like smoke rising from the tapers recently flameless wick. Was it the vision of a celebratory ghost or just the kind of merriment one has upon a bottle of sherry?

Journal Entry for Monday, December 27, 1841
Did not see the ghost of Archibald Frew for the remainder of the Christmas holiday season. As he had never given me occasion to be frightened of his presence, I dare to say I missed the old chap. His playfulness about the Christmas tree was most engaging.

Journal Entry for Saturday, February 5, 1842

The winter this season has been especially harsh. The temperatures have been consistently below what I believe the usual numbers to be. Icicles dangle like swords from nearly every tree limb and a heavy layer of frost covers every windowpane. The fog from the north is rolling like clouds across the lawn, and yet, I, from the doorway of my room, can see something swirling in the dankness. Something odd is indeed happening out on the lawn. As the swirls of fog encircled the oak tree, I began to see that the patterns in the fog appear to be arranged as if some figure were walking through, but no person is there. Then, as if by magic, footprints appear in the snow that covers the grass. Only footprints appear, leaving their maker in a shroud of dense fog. Is it my imagination? Is there a person wandering through the winter air? This I cannot say for sure, only that there is a presence here today. Fog envelopes the estate.

Journal Entry for Thursday, April 18, 1850

As I have previously mentioned in this journal, I have continued to see what I believe to be the ghost of prior owner Archibald Frew. I saw his figure again today. I have assigned no menacing character traits to him. He seems like an affable fellow, more concerned with admiring his plantation than with frightening away its current occupants. In fact, I think he may be unaware that he himself is even dead. I am not convinced he knows that he is in the spirit world. He seems engaged only in the property and items that were here on the day of his death. The ghost has never tried to engage with me, nor I with him directly. I noted in a prior entry that Dr. Caldwell has now himself begun to make note that there is some presence, but he and I have not settled on a conversation over the matter. For example, this afternoon, I heard Dr. Caldwell shout across the house for his wife to quit playing the piano. The noise was distracting to him during his work. The two of them seemed equally surprised when she came in from the herb garden to ask what he was shouting for. If it was not Mrs. Caldwell playing the piano, who was it? I suspect, though I would never question Dr. Caldwell, it was Archibald Frew. The notes, though distant, were of a funeral dirge.

Journal Entry for Monday, July 17, 1854

I have heard in days past that the slaves working in the kitchen and house have experienced encounters with those of the spirit world. I had not stopped to consider those encounters for myself as the slaves have their own culture and set of beliefs and it is not my place to concern myself with their stories. However, I have heard the slaves speak of spiritual sensations, I would say

27: Rosedale Plantation

The servants' area in the basement of Rosedale.

visions—but these may be more my interpretations than their actual intentions—within the house and grounds.

They, in fact, have spoken at length about sensing the presence of apparitions in the lower quarters where the cooking fireplace is. In the cellar below the main floor, there is a preparation table and a fireplace where many of the meals are cooked. I have heard talk that there is a presence over the preparation table. The slaves themselves think it is some sort of spirit that blesses the food and imbues it with goodness. I do not use the word goodness in the sense of taste, but in the sense of spiritual goodness, free from iniquities. It is my understanding that the slaves brought to the plantation have all manner of supernatural perception, and so a connection to the spirit world seems to come to them more through grace than deliberate seeking. I suspect, also, the spirit sensations felt by the slaves in the cook area of the cellar are just as real to them as my visions of Archibald Frew are to me. I do not question, in the least, the legitimacy of their claims that the slave quarters are haunted by the spirits of the slaves who died on this plantation. We all, slave or free, acknowledge our ancestors of a past generation.

Journal Entry for Tuesday, August 15, 1854

Although I have written in this record several times about the visions I have had of the prior owner Archibald Frew, it is today that I write in regards to another ghoul. One that seems to have taken to lurking about the small brick well house, or outbuilding, just beyond the Shegaw Creek Presbyterian Church that sits adjacent to Rosedale. I was collecting berries in the wooded area near the church when a strange ghoul reached its hand, or what I thought was a hand, over the roof of the building. It lunged itself up onto the roof and waved furiously at the sky. As it waved its arm about, lightning bolts cracked the humid day. It was something out of the nightmares of poet Edgar Allen Poe. Not quite a gargoyle in its shape, it was not exactly human either. It was astonishing in its wrath—cold, a seething like the wild fancies of some agitated beast. It frightened me a great deal and I ran back to the house as quickly as I could run. It did not follow me, but I am shaking my quill about in trepidation of its re-appearance. I feel safe back at the house, but I will not venture over to the outbuilding again without my rifle.

Was it real? It aroused in me a feeling of wild sensibilities, not just a thing to behold with my eyes. Did some grotesque thing leer at me? Alternatively, is it all in an overactive imagination? On the other hand, perhaps it is a sign of things to come. I know not what to make of it, and now find myself feeling foolish for my fright at the outbuilding. I hope I can sleep tonight in peace, and that tomorrow's light will bring me back to my normal senses.

Journal Entry for Saturday, August 19, 1854

My nerves are still somewhat unwound from the incident last Tuesday near the church outbuilding. I have not seen the ghoulish gray thing again, although my mind wields its thoughts at any shrill moment. I have prayed in the last five days like I have never prayed before. I pray to be kept safe, both from the beast and from my own thoughts of that frightening creature.

Journal Entry for Wednesday, October 24, 1855

It has been over a year since I last saw anything at the Rosedale Plantation that I might describe here as supernatural. After the sighting of the ghoul on the outbuilding, I relished in some quiet time. I pulled out the journal tonight only to say that I have again sensed something beyond what most would call regular. In the late afternoon hours this day, I saw as clearly as I have ever seen the ghost of Archibald Frew. Again, he pleasantly roamed past where I stood, only this time I got the distinct feeling that, for the first time, he looked over my way and he saw me. He, at least I think, sensed my

27: Rosedale Plantation

A bedroom at Rosedale, with what appears to be a ghostly figure at the door.

presence in his world. It was as if we somehow acknowledged each other in a fashion we had not previously been at liberty to enjoy before.

Journal Entry for Monday, November 29, 1858
As I have alluded to several times before in this very journal, I have been in some strange sort of contact with a man named Archibald Frew. This would be of little matter, other than the fact that Mr. Frew has been dead these many years. I have seen him, though, around the grounds and in the house a number of times since I first arrived here almost twenty years ago. At first, I was only able to see him in a mist or fog. As time carried on, I was able to see him more clearly, and he was better able to interact with his surroundings. Lately, though, as things have gotten tenser due to what I am afraid is a coming battle, he has become even more, shall we say, animated. I find myself, now, in the odd predicament of being able to interact with him on a limited basis. I wonder if he can feel the war that I am afraid might happen to this delicate nation. The papers have been saying, for some weeks now, that some southern states may withdraw from the union of states. I do hope it is idle speculation on the part of the newspapers. However, spirits, can, I believe, sense things that we cannot, and yet I am not in disharmony with Mr. Archibald Frew's concerns for the future security of this plantation. I would never say that the two of us have conversed in the normal manner,

Haunted Charlotte

The piano in the living room.

nevertheless, we exchange glances that to me imply, "You will help, will not you?" to me. I would be led to think that Archibald Frew would like me to help him, somehow, to save his beloved plantation. What am I, a lowly gardener, to do? This here ends the journal entry for this date.

> *An odd thing has happened. A thing of most egregious shock, the revelation was! Today, Thursday, March 1, 1860, I went to the bookshelf to retrieve the journal that was serving as a record for the supernatural occurrences around the Rosedale Plantation. I had been under the strictest belief that I alone was the sole scriber and reader of the journal. I was simply keeping it for my own remembrances, and perhaps amusement. When, though, today I went to pull it off the shelf, it fell from my hands and landed open on the floor before my feet. It was open to the last page I had written in some weeks prior. I was taken aghast to learn that I was not the last person to have written in the pages of the journal. At first, I simply looked at the words that were not in my own hand, staring in amazement. Would another reader think me unsuitable for employment, for freedom itself, if the reader had come to realize my relationship with a ghost? No, upon inspection of the alternate writer's words, I have come to the conclusion that they will not think me mad. Madness is not the conclusion they would come to…*

27: Rosedale Plantation

Journal Entry for Monday, October 23, 1859

I happen to know that this journal was in the ownership of the Rosedale Plantation gardener, a man by the name of Theodore Kratz, and that it shall go to his family upon the reading of his will, if there is one. I have written here now to make record for his family, with sincere apologies for the invasion of his privacy. Mr. Kratz went to heaven to be with the king of kings today. He made his heavenly ascent at 2:20 in the afternoon hours on this date. He had been sick from pneumonia since winter last, nearly a year now. May his soul rest in peace, and his family find comfort in the good work he did here on earth in his 34 years.

28
The Shotgun Houses

"The Shotgun Houses" in Northeast Charlotte only seem peaceful today.

28: The Shotgun Houses

The clearly visible underside of the left "Shotgun House" is reputed to be haunted by some sort of creature.

Known locally as "The Shotgun Houses," the strange, white clapboard homes sit oddly on a misshapen lot on the northeast side of uptown Charlotte. Their precise history is lost to eternity, but what we do know about them is that they are haunted. Thought to have been slave or servant quarters for those working for the society class in Charlotte, "The Shotgun Houses" are home to several spirits and the location of a number of strange stories.

The most retold story about "The Shotgun Houses" is that they were once located on another lot and that they were moved to their current location sometime in the mid-20th century. As the legend goes, a young boy by the name of Josiah died in the left house from unknown causes sometime before they were moved. When they were re-located, his spirit was split between where they had been and where they are now. This forced removal of a place of haunting has caused the spirit to become torn. It seems that "half" his spirit occupies the house, while part of him remains missing in another location. As a result of this spirit split, what remains of Josiah can be sensed repeatedly walking out the front door and moving off the property, only to be captured in a cycle of yearning to be re-united with his other half.

Another prominent spirit that occupies "The Shotgun Houses" is that of a little girl who most likely died of yellow fever in the home at the end of the 19th century. Several visitors to the houses have reported that they have seen a little African-American girl playing on the porch. She seems blissfully unaware of her surroundings, and simply continues to play with her dolls on the porch. Upon being approached, she vanishes into the illusive ether of some other space.

In addition to the aforementioned spirits, one story from the pages of "The Shotgun Houses'" strange history is what has become known as "the beast beneath." According to legend, a supernatural beast lives in the space under the homes. The descriptions of the creature vary wildly, and no two people have reported the same thing. Paranormal investigators call this phenomena "shapeshifting." The only consistent thread in the descriptions of the beast is that it is not human in form. Not visible in the daylight hours, the creature can be seen emanating odd shades of spectral light from underneath the house on the right. The down-turned floorboards that make up the ceiling of the crawl space are said to have once been turned upright, once being the floor of the main level. According to police reports, there was a brutal murder in the right house some years back. The crew assigned to clean up simply turned the blood stained planks over to reveal the clean side. Some suspect this blood feeds or is related to "the beast beneath."

Conclusion

…and as you close the coffin lid on this collection of stories…be sure to look over your shoulder, for one never knows what may be lurking around in Charlotte's haunted history. North Carolina's largest city, Charlotte is known for the paranormal residue that can be revealed in its cemeteries, houses, buildings, and beyond. Come visit Charlotte, and witness for yourself the supernatural stories that the Queen City has to offer.
…Come along….but not alone.

Spooky Gallery

Spectral image photographed inside the Mecklenburg County Courthouse.

Paranormal investigation of Old Elmwood Cemetery.

Ghostly image captured during paranormal investigation of Town Square in Matthews.

Bridge near Charlotte said to be haunted.

Anna Leigh Wellper's former play room.

Author Roy Heizer conducting a Ghost Tour.